Kingd
Perspe
SERIE

CW00732511

Citizens OF THE Kingdom

REVEALING THE TRUE COST
OF DISCIPLESHIP

Alan J. Osborn

Book Series website is www.kingdomperspective.net
Published by Osborn Publishing, Ramsgate, England
Cover Design by Annika Mai Kreitsman

ISBN 978-1-913858-02-5

First Edition, Revision A. First Printed in England November, 2021.

Dedication

This book is dedicated to

Alice

Acknowledgements

Much of the resource used in part two of this series has of course been the guiding and inspiration of the Holy Spirit, but there are some particular people to highlight and honour...

Geoff Richardson. If it wasn't for your 'yes' of acceptance to my Bible College application, this book series would probably never have been written. Not only that, but you always spoke the 'truth in love' to stretch and grow me throughout my time at Regents. And now, even during your retirement years, you still are willing to pass on your wisdom, knowledge and vast breadth of experience. I know that I am not the only one that you have discipled. Thank you.

Peter Haycock. Thank you for your time, energy and effort in reading through and giving detailed feedback on the first draft. Your seeing things through a slightly different lens has helped me greatly.

Chris and Steph Aaron. I wanted to acknowledge and thank you for your support that has come in other ways. I truly value our friendship and walking as disciples together.

Those who discipled me. There are many people who have influenced my Christian life greatly, probably too many to mention. A few that I must though are: John and Trish Waller, the late Rowland Bell, Bruce and Sharon Oliver, Nadya Dyett, Nick Whittome, Alan Poole, Rafael Gutiérrez, Dave Campbell and John Glass.

Those that I discipled. You will know if you have been one of my disciples. I pray that you will have experienced my heart for you and wanting to see you develop, grow and become all that you can be in Jesus.

Preface

This second book in the Kingdom Perspective Series is part of a broader four-part work, that covers the four components of any and every kingdom. It is my hope and prayer that each book will be a helpful stand-alone resource to the Body of Christ, at the same time, retaining its vital part in the broader understanding of living from a 'Kingdom Perspective'. In other words, each book will be an important, individual piece in a four-piece jigsaw.

In my first book, '*Territory of the Kingdom*', I proposed a framework to enable us to see more clearly the magnitude and the magnificence of what we inherit when we choose to follow Jesus, how his Kingdom functions, and how we, as those upon whom Jesus conferred his Kingdom, are to operate in it.

This book, '*Citizens of the Kingdom*', aims to help us see what it will actually cost us to truly follow Jesus and be one of his disciples. This is summed up perfectly by the late German Theologian Dietrich Bonhoeffer... **"Salvation is free, but discipleship will cost you your life"**.[1] The Kingdom must be formed within us as disciples of Jesus so that its influence can be extended through us. And so, we will look at both what our 'no cost' salvation means, as well the high price we have to pay to live as a disciple. Later to follow will come a book on the '*Laws of the Kingdom*' and then finally, the '*King of the Kingdom*'.

---

[1] Bonhoeffer, D. *The Cost of Discipleship* (London: SCM Press, 1959).

The number one topic that Jesus spoke about and that he also demonstrated was his Kingdom. My desire through this series is to help take something that seems either complex, often misunderstood or somehow hidden from our understanding, and bring it with a new level of clarity, to the forefront of our thinking, so that **the main thing Jesus spoke about, becomes the main thing that we speak about and that we demonstrate**.

When I learnt about these four (aforementioned) components of any and every kingdom, they suddenly allowed me to see a way of framing things with greater clarity. This also enabled me to begin my own journey of discovery into each one. I had no idea where this would take me or what the results would be, either for me personally or for the church I lead. Yet, it seemed to be the right direction in which to head. I use the words *disciple*, *citizen* and *subject* synonymously throughout this book.

It cost me nothing to be a UK citizen, but I must act responsibly, follow the laws of this land, and pay my taxes. It cost me nothing to have the title of a 'disciple of Jesus' or a 'citizen of the Kingdom', but to truly live as one will cost everything that I am and all that I have. I do hope and pray that this book will inspire you to consider the great cost to your own life in truly following Jesus. Christianity is easy enough to accept, but to develop into your true potential, to live this greatest adventure to its maximum, is not for the faint-hearted. However, it is only as we look to discover the depth of meaning of our salvation, that our motivation for living in the Kingdom as one of its citizens is established.

I am still journeying and still learning! I may never be able to fully grasp all that the Kingdom is and means, but I'm enjoying the adventure and felt that it could be helpful for you to be able to see with a 'Kingdom Perspective' also.

I have at least now discovered one important thing: that I must preach the Kingdom... *"Jesus said, "I must preach the good news of the Kingdom of God to the other towns also, **because that is why I was sent**""* (Luke 4:43).

Foreword

We first met Alan in 1989, when, straight out of Bible College, we moved to Slough in Berkshire to take up our first pastorate. It was a new church plant as part of the Kensington Temple satellite programme. A group of around fifteen of us met on Sunday evenings in a rented hall. Alan and his small family came along on week two, and on the next Sunday, Alan decided to become a disciple of Jesus Christ. What a privilege for us to be with Alan from day one of him becoming a Christian, and becoming a part of the Kingdom.

Over the years our lives took us in different directions. We left Slough to take up missions work in West Africa, from there to Ireland and then back to London. But throughout those years we seemed to cross paths again and again. With a young family to support, Alan had to work full time but never shied away from his Kingdom responsibilities and the call of God on his life. He worked hard to develop his musical skills to enable him to lead worship. He rose to the challenge of leading the church when there was no full-time minister. He found time to undertake theological studies and also took part in overseas mission trips.

At a time in his life when things should have been easier, he answered the call to full-time ministry. After being part of a team in Lane End, near High Wycombe in Buckinghamshire, he was then appointed Senior Minister in Elim Oasis Church in Broadstairs, Kent. As this series of books on the Kingdom show, even this responsibility hasn't quenched his thirst for more of God for himself, and for others.

Citizens of the Kingdom, the second in a four-part series of books, is designed to help the reader understand the true cost of becoming a disciple of Jesus. Salvation and all that it encompasses is clearly spelt out in the opening section of the book. But as we see, salvation is not the end but rather the beginning of a truly amazing journey with Jesus if only we give ourselves wholeheartedly to obeying and following him. Alan likens our walk with the Lord to being an "apprenticeship". None of us knows everything when we become citizens of the Kingdom. We all need to learn and to grow and this takes time.

This book is not designed as a fast track to perfect citizenship. Rather it takes us through the various skills we need to develop our relationship with God. Some may be obvious, i.e. we know we should attend meetings and pray, but what about fasting, service and total commitment?

We could tell many stories of Alan's early years as a citizen. The challenges he faced would have overwhelmed many seasoned believers. He was steadfast in doing what he knew God wanted from him and he didn't buckle under pressure. For this reason, he is highly qualified to tackle the subject of this book. He has lived it and knows it is the only way. All or nothing!

Whether reading this as an individual or as part of a small group, it will challenge your thinking, your attitudes and your commitment to Jesus and his Kingdom. Therefore, we highly recommend it to you.

Rev. John and Trish Waller

Contents

SECTION ONE

Are you really a Disciple?

CHAPTER ONE

What Happens When You Are Saved?

I remember one day when my son Carl was about nine years old and we were holidaying and out walking in the scenic Lake District, in the North West of England. As he, his younger sister Sasha and I attempted to cross a small river, by bounding across some very large rocks that sat just above the surface of the water, he slipped off and tumbled in. Now whilst this river was not particularly wide nor very deep, it was powerful and fast-moving because we were not too far from a waterfall! Fortunately, there was another natural line of very large rocks in the river about ten meters downstream, that happened to have another group out walking and also crossing the river using that set of rocks. A man from that group saw what had happened and he was able to grab Carl, who was slipping closer and faster towards the waterfall, and haul him out of the water. He rescued my son. He saved him.

What does it mean when Christians use terms like 'to save' or 'saved'? Save just means to keep safe or to rescue, someone or something, from harm or danger. Saved is the past tense. When disciples of Jesus ask questions like "are you saved?" or "are they saved?", or make statements like "I was saved five years ago", they are referring to being rescued. Rescued from the penalty of their wrongdoing or sin. I'll try to keep the explanation of that rescue short and simple in this chapter.

Sin, which is anything at all that does not line up with God's purposes or breaks his standards,[2] entered into this world that God had created perfectly, through the original or first sin of both Adam and Eve. God gave them the free choice, which we still have today, but 'strongly recommended!' that when they were in the Garden of Eden, not to eat of the forbidden fruit so that they would remain innocent of the knowledge of evil. This could be achieved by simply not eating from just one tree in a paradisical garden, that was full of trees hanging with all kinds of delicious fruit. They both ate. The result being that everyone is now born contaminated by sin and is inclined to sin.[3]

Health and Safety

Why? Why would God not want humanity to find this out for themselves? Well God seems to set a standard here of what is acceptable and what is not. He is a creator God who knows all things including what is best for the people he creates. He is therefore wanting to provide safety limits for their lives in order to keep them from getting hurt. God continues in this vein, to set the direction in and for our lives today – and we can choose, and should choose, to obey him both for our benefit and for the benefit of others.

Placement

Earlier, before this notoriously poor choice had been made, even before Eve had arrived on the scene, it was God who created the garden environment and put Adam in it to tend it.

---

[2] Warrington, K. *Pentecostal Theology. A Theology of Encounter* (London: T & T Clark, 2008), P35.
[3] Ibid.

God 'puts us' into certain places today, to train and develop us, to help us grow as people, just like he did with Adam. So where is it exactly that God has put you, in your family, church, social life, job, university and in your circle of friends? Whatever places you find yourself in, God has put you there to enable you to make the choices necessary to deal with the things of your own heart.

Do you like where God has put you? Is it a great place to be? Some might answer yes, but probably not all of you. The Bible does not tell us if Adam did or didn't actually like to garden. Nevertheless, if it is a difficult or uncomfortable place that you are currently in, the questions remain: are you willing to change? and are you willing to grow? God has made you for great purpose and given you things to do and to learn along the journey that is your life.

Connected Obedience

In this season when it was just Adam and God, Adam remained obedient. Prior to Eve's sensational arrival, Adam had been given privileges, responsibilities and also authority to carry out certain tasks. God will have some specific and special tasks that are just for you, that help you grow and that will have the added benefit of extending the influence of his Kingdom. Do you know what his tasks for you are, what he has called you to do, and are you doing them? It can be easy to forget that we are privileged sons and daughters of the living God, that we have responsibilities and tasks given to us, and that we walk in the authority given or conferred on us by Jesus. Adam's story is a reminder to us.

Your purpose is to change and become the best you can be, and to continue on the path God has for you as closely as you possibly can. Entering into a loving and therefore obedient relationship with a God that is alive and well, means a change of life's focus to develop that connection with him above all else.

The Great Separation

Since the point in history when Adam and Eve allowed sin to enter this world, as a consequence (and boy don't we know that our choices really do have consequences), humanity is born into this world physically but is separated from God spiritually. That is just the way it is I'm afraid. God is Holy and cannot otherwise be, whilst people are inclined to sin and do things their own way. So, there is a problem! How can an unholy or 'sinful people' get back into relationship with a Holy God? Well, the answer is through his Son Jesus who was holy and without sin, because **he always made the choice to live with and in obedience to his Father**. Jesus became a perfect sacrifice and covering for everyone's sin – which is the really good news story: the Gospel! Please note though, that God's amazing grace to us is not a license to sin because they have all been forgiven, but rather is a realisation that we are called to live evermore holy lives.

The Great Rescue

When that unsung hero saved Carl, he didn't need a reward or payment for helping – he just helped. Can you imagine if he had shouted upstream... "give me £10,000 and I will save your son!" He didn't, he simply helped, and so would we. God has done the same thing. Through Adam and Eve's poor choice the human race became sinful by default and therefore separated from this Holy God. But God is cleverer than us! He knows everything anyway and he always had a rescue plan in mind. He would send a 'man' that happened to be his own Son to this earth, in the most incredible way, to rescue people from their sin. To save them, and to save us too.

That's not the end of the story. The man at the river rescued Carl and at the same time he also therefore physically preserved life. Jesus came to rescue, but that also means to give something else: to give life! God, through Jesus, rescues, or saves, and preserves our lives, but there is more! Can you believe it? More you ask? Yes. Jesus also came to transform your life into a life of fullness or abundance, to make you 'spiritually alive' and able to have an ongoing relationship with God, reversing the impact of the first-ever sin and providing the solution to humanity's biggest problem. Wow, that's amazing I hear you say. But not only that! This new spiritual connection with God becomes eternal. Eternal life in paradise with him! No wonder it's called the Gospel or the good news story.

Therefore, we are rescued, made spiritually alive and also connected with God, now in the present, and spending eternity with him in paradise in the future. And it is all free. This is what it means to be saved! It is what this world is crying out for you to tell them.

Where's the catch you might ask. There is just one. Jesus is the only perfect sacrifice for sin, and to indeed have all these things that he freely provides – to be saved – you must believe in him, and allow him into your life as your King or Lord. This means that he rules in all that you do, as you become his 'subject', his disciple, part of the Bride of Christ, the global Church, and a citizen of his Kingdom. I will use three terms, *disciple*, *citizen*, and *subject* synonymously throughout this book.

Jesus becomes your Saviour from the justifiable penalty of your wrongdoing, your sin. He is the only person who remained holy and is able to save. All of this is a free act, a step of trust that you take, by choosing to put your faith in the only person who can. Jesus saves you, loves you, and wants to transform your life into one of real purpose.

Do you wish to believe in Jesus this way? Then 'confess' or tell someone else that this is the decision you have made and you will be saved (Rom. 10:9). Jesus came with a message... "*repent for the Kingdom of Heaven is at hand*" (Matt. 4:17). Repent means to turn from going your way, to going God's way for your life. **We repent towards God**. It is a complete 180-degree U-turn in which we place our faith in Jesus. **We believe in Jesus**, that he sacrificially died for our sin and was resurrected – overcoming death. His Kingdom is available for free on this earth right now and is the Kingdom you will live in, in the future – forever. This offer is unbeatable! When we accept it, a heavenly transaction takes place and you begin to be able to experience God, through the gift of the Holy Spirit. **We receive the Spirit**. From experiencing his love, you are then to love and obey God above all else (Deut. 6:5-9). God the Father, Son and Holy Spirit must then be at the centre of everything in your life.

If anyone reading this has never made that step of repenting towards God, believing in Jesus and receiving the Spirit, and would like this amazing free gift of new life, then please pray this rescue prayer with me. It simply helps make it a genuine heartfelt decision...

Jesus, I now recognise that I have lived my life my way and on my terms without you. I see how you have been drawing me to yourself and I now choose to make the decision to believe that you are God's Son, that you died for my wrong doing. I decide to turn towards you, God, and to believe in you, Jesus, and put my faith in you. I turn from living my way and invite you to be my very real God and to dwell inside of me, through the Holy Spirit. I want to make you the Lord or ruler of my life, that I might know you, follow you and grow to be your disciple so that my life will make a difference for you and your Kingdom on this earth. Amen.

I know that many will rightly point out that no such prayer is found in the New Testament (NT), and that simply getting people to say this prayer will not make a disciple of anyone. I agree. Such a prayer is only just the beginning of a new life that walks with Jesus. Discipleship can never be an optional extra, as Jesus calls people to live a completely new life.[4] I would add though, that neither are the words we would say at a wedding ceremony. We say them and mean them as a promise before God...and then the real work starts! For the rest of our lives, we commit to building a healthy and loving marriage. This is how I see the rescue prayer.

---

[4] Hull, B., Sobels, B. *The Discipleship Gospel. What Jesus preached – we must follow* (USA: Harrington Interactive Media (HIM) Publications, 2018), P38.

Jesus' own upbringing would have followed the rhythm of the Jewish calendar and God's law (the Torah), because Israel's religion and culture were completely entwined, whereas today in Western culture this generally is not the case.[5] In Jewish culture, to live a life that is pleasing to God, meant to discuss how God's commands should be interpreted and lived out in their community. The Talmud contains the teachings of the most important rabbis over many centuries. The English word disciple is translated from Greek, that in turn is translated from the Hebrew word *talmid*, meaning student. A talmid is not only to learn from a rabbi, but **to become like him in every way**. Therefore, we don't become Christian through a prayer alone, that is just our choice to begin to follow the rabbi Jesus. If salvation is the door, discipleship is the ongoing journey we then enter into.[6]

Before we made this prayerful step, the Holy Spirit will have been drawing us towards God, but now at salvation, he resides within us. We have incredibly gained access to the Father, Son and Holy Spirit. **As new citizens of God's Kingdom, we choose to go the way of the Kingdom consistently and with every decision we make**. God's Kingdom should now become our first priority as we seek it (Matt. 6:33) through relationship with our King.

---

[5] Hoffbrand, D. *The Jewish Jesus. Reconnecting with the truth about Jesus, Israel, & the Church* (Shippensburg: Destiny Image Publishers Inc., 2017), P38.
[6] Ibid, P46-7.

Repentance and faith are not one-off things but they should become part of our new lifestyle. They provide the first two of four wheels needed for a car to move forward if that example is helpful. The other two wheels are found in baptism. Firstly, a baptism of believers in water, by full immersion or getting 'dunked', and secondly, through baptism or being fully immersed, 'drenched', or overflowing with the Holy Spirit. I believe these baptisms 'seal the deal' as it were, like a legal transaction, but in the spiritual realm.

The Holy Spirit baptism can occur at the point we are saved, but often it comes subsequently through another prayer. This was my own experience. The Spirit was drawing me over a couple of years and then at salvation I was indwelt by him, with that cleansing or newness of life, which confirmed to me that I had met Jesus and was saved. Two months later I was prayed for and received the baptism in the Holy Spirit and spoke in tongues. Instead of only a residing Holy Spirit, we can seek this full immersion in him, so that we can be empowered to walk this journey of faith. Something that is also free! My water baptism came around four months later.

These four wheels of repentance, faith, water baptism and Holy Spirit baptism – help us to move forward as a disciple of Jesus and in the work of his Kingdom. If any one of these four wheels is missing, just like a car, we too can get stuck in our journey of discipleship. It will be for your benefit to speak with a more mature disciple or a church leader, and head in for a pit stop to get any missing wheel fixed.

At the point of salvation, there is unfortunately no 'reset' or 'reboot' that takes place within us, to deal with all the negative effects sin may have had upon us. We gain new spiritual life, but the area of our soul, the person within, has built up behaviours or coping mechanisms to get us through this life, because of the hurtful things that either we have done or have been done to us. Therefore, we need to journey closely with Jesus to be able to discover true freedom. Jesus is the truth that is able to set us free... "*Jesus said, "If you hold to my teaching, you are really my disciples. Then you will know the truth, and the truth will set you free*"" (John 8:31b-32). If we allow the Holy Spirit access into the very core of our being, he will begin to make these changes step by step for the remainder of our lives as we become more like Jesus. This is the beautiful adventure that is in store for all those who are citizens of the Kingdom.

Back in the river where Carl was rescued, one final thing took place. Both Sasha and I were rescued from the devastation of tremendous grief. I don't think we could imagine life without him. For some of you though, your story may not have been as fortunate as ours. My point is that God did not spare his only Son so that you could be rescued – it did cost them both dearly – and God does feel this same loss and grief when any person that he created is not rescued. Our rescue story truly is an incredible one, and we now get to play a small part in the rescue of others.

CHAPTER TWO

Delving Deeper into Salvation

For those who have already made the decision to become a disciple of Jesus, I wanted to dig a little deeper to show what else happens when we are 'saved', so that we can be encouraged and amazed all over again at what God has done for us. If this has been a recent decision for you, perhaps even at the end of the previous chapter, then I hope that this second chapter 'blows your socks off', as you better grasp the greatness of what has just happened, of your salvation.

When we have been disciples of Jesus for a while, we can unintentionally take these most incredible truths for granted. Isn't it true that we often chase hard after incredible or seemingly impossible things until eventually we gain them? When we do, we are overjoyed and feel proud and blessed. Perhaps it was something as simple as the latest phone. You desired it and you worked and saved until you could buy it or could afford the repayment plan on it. When it arrived you carefully opened the box and got to touch and hold it for the first time. It was almost a sacred thing, a holy phone moment! Fast forward a few months and it has lost its glowing appeal now that you have found out its new features are only 'nice'. It has gained some scratches and a newer model is soon due. It has become ordinary again. This is what can happen, and unfortunately often does happen, with our own rescue.

Sometimes our focus can move elsewhere, as we get so busy doing the tasks that God has given us, and sometimes tasks that he hasn't. It is worth taking time here to be reminded all over again why it is that we are serving in all the ways that we do. There may perhaps be some new words in here for you, but I will do my best to make them clear and understandable. First though, an inspirational list!

We are...
- delivered or rescued from mortality and death, the penalty of sin;
- forgiven from all sin past, present and future;
- redeemed – our un-payable debt is cancelled;
- purified from sin and made clean on the inside;
- reconciled to the Father;
- given the right standing or positioning before God, by gaining the righteousness of Jesus;
- brought into relationship with Father, Son and Spirit;
- made alive in Christ;
- united with Christ;
- ambassadors of Christ;
- sealed and anointed by the Holy Spirit;
- made a completely new creation.

We have...
- Jesus' ways being formed within us by the Holy Spirit;
- gained eternal life;
- become free;
- had our guilt and shame removed;
- been born spiritually as the Holy Spirit indwells us;
- a share in the life, death and resurrection of Jesus;
- divine acquittal on judgement day.

I could go on, but let's get on with the task of unpacking the deeper truths of our salvation, starting with the first of seven words: *atonement*. By the way, in the Psalms, there is often found the word '*Selah*' which means to pause, to wait or to reflect. I will add this after each of our seven words so that you can do just that.

Atonement

The word atone means to make amends for something wrong that you did or even for something that you failed to do. In Old Testament (OT) times they held to an animal sacrificial system to do this, to say sorry and to also appease God's penalty for people's sin. To wash away the sin from people was not free. Sin was taken very seriously and people would bring their best animals (without any blemishes and of the highest monetary value), that were sacrificed to make things right again before their Holy God. The problem was though, that they kept on sinning, and so therefore this animal slaughter became a perpetual need. Its purpose was to allow sinful people to approach him.[7]

In Jewish culture there is an annual 'Day of Atonement', in which the high priest enters into the Holy of Holies (or God's dwelling place within the Temple), with the blood from an animal sacrifice, to atone for the whole nation's sin. This takes place ten days after the Jewish New Year and is a day of prayer and fasting, with no food or drink. An animal **without defect** is required to be offered in this sacrifice.

---

[7] Boice, J. M. *Foundations of the Christian Faith. A Comprehensive & Readable Theology* (Downers Grove: Inter-Varsity Press, 1986), P313.

Can you imagine a modern developed nation ever doing this – a day in which the whole nation neither eats nor drinks and everyone spends the day in prayer? Even in the Covid-19 pandemic, the UK government did not declare a National Day of Prayer and fasting, despite well over a hundred thousand losing their lives. I imagine that they saw this as being the job of the church to whom the responsibility is outsourced. Church movements and denominations did this, but the Christian Church only counts for around 6-8% of the population. I do wonder what it would take for a government to ever now suggest this.

As we have seen, mankind is born into a world that contains sin. The Fall, or original sin, meant that all of humanity is born physically alive, but spiritually dead. Therefore, by default, the world sits under God's wrath and judgment because he is holy. The atonement deals with this precarious position that we find ourselves in, for any who would choose to accept Jesus. This is where God stepped in. He himself never did anything wrong and had nothing to be sorry for, but in his grace and mercy offered his most precious Jesus to atone for our wrongdoing. Jesus' sacrificial death demonstrates God's supreme love for mankind as he provided the most costly way, the death of his one and only **perfect and sinless Son**, to pay the penalty that our sin demands... "*God was in Christ reconciling the world to himself*" (2 Cor. 5:19).

Jesus was without sin... "*God made him who had no sin to be sin for us, so that in him we might become the righteousness of God*" (2 Cor. 5:21a), his sacrificial death was once, and for all of humanity. This deals with both the issue of sin and the judgment that it attracts. His shed blood accomplished so much, more than the shedding of animal's blood and applying or sprinkling it on things, which was another part of this OT praxis. This does all seem a little strange today for those of us not living in that time and culture, doesn't it? But think about it for a moment: life flow is found in our blood, and applying it by sprinkling it on something was to apply life to that thing and not death. We have the medical advances today to allow those who are skilled to do so to give blood transfusions, and these bring us life and save us from death. As Jesus shed his blood, which was both perfect and divine, while he himself died, he was applying life upon humanity... *"I have been crucified with Christ and I no longer live, but Christ lives in me. The life I now live in the body, I live by faith in the Son of God, who loved me and gave himself for me"* (Gal. 2:20). He was making both new life and eternal life available... *"the gift of God is eternal life in Christ Jesus our Lord"* (Rom. 6:23b). His blood offering to God the Father was an offering of life.

From the writings of the Apostle Paul, Ladd notes that *"in almost every letter Paul refers in one form or another to the death of Christ"*.[8] He does so with varying expressions like Christ's death, cross, crucifixion or blood[9] – a sacrificial death indeed. The life of Jesus was released to all people in the form of his blood, which liberates us and sets us free.

---

[8] Ladd, G. E. *A Theology of the New Testament* (Grand Rapids: William B. Eerdmans Publishing Company, 1974), P423.
[9] Ibid.

God's love and justice are the cause of the atonement. He did not have to save anyone but decided to, through the suffering and death of his willing and obedient Son,[10] making us to be at one or in harmony with him. Atonement therefore refers to the forgiving or pardoning of all our sin, through the suffering, the death and the resurrection of Jesus (Rom. 6:5, 8).

Selah.

Vicarious

Vicarious essentially means that we indirectly experience the activities done by another, rather than doing those activities ourselves. We don't, therefore, have to face the penalty of our sin because Jesus has taken care of that for us. Phew!

Jesus died for us... "*God demonstrates His own love toward us, in that while we were still sinners, Christ died for us*" (Rom. 5:8), so that we could be 'saved'... "*for God did not appoint us to suffer wrath but to receive salvation through our Lord Jesus Christ*" (1 Thes. 5:9). Jesus gave his life for us as a ransom... "*for even the Son of Man did not come to be served, but to serve, and to give his life as a ransom for many*" (Mark 10:45), and... "*for there is one God and one mediator between God and mankind, the man Christ Jesus, who gave himself as a ransom for all people*" (1 Tim. 2:5-6a).

Jesus chose to come under the blight, disease or curse of sin and to take its condition upon himself, including its penalty...

---

[10] Grudem, W. *Systematic Theology. An Introduction to Biblical Doctrine* (Leicester: Inter-Varsity Press, 1994), P569-70.

"for the wages of sin is death" (Rom. 6:23a), which meant that he would have to die and that during this awful process he would also be temporarily separated from God... *"My God, my God, why have you forsaken me?"* (Matt. 27:46b), which shows his sacrificial physical death.

When vicarious is offered by the offended party, in this case God, it is the highest form of mercy.[11] In fact a vicar stands in place of and represents another; Jesus too stood in our place, represented us and took our death penalty.[12]

Selah.

Isn't this all so incredible? Considering we have only looked at two words so far: atonement and vicarious. There are another five that I'd like to explore, making seven in all – the number for perfection.

Substitutionary

We probably all know that in sports there are substitutes. These are people on the team who remain sat on the benches or side line, hoping and waiting with anticipation to become a part of the game. Perhaps someone will underperform or sustain an injury and need to be replaced, or a tactical change might be made by the manager or coach, to better exploit a weakness in the opposing team. Everyone longs to be in the game, the substitutes are watching carefully and wanting to get the

---

[11] Berkhof, L. *Systematic Theology* (Edinburgh: The Banner of Truth Trust, 1958), P375-6.

[12] Grudem, W. *Systematic Theology*, P579.

chance to prove themselves. The people on the field would rather stay there if possible but realise they could be taken off for the benefit of the whole team. I can remember back in my younger years watching the top football teams in England and a certain team, almost without fail, would bring on a particular substitute player in the last part of the game, who would inevitably score and turn the game around to win. They would bring on their super-sub!

With its default position of living in a world that contains sin, humanity is losing the game. In fact, they have no chance of possibly winning, they need a miracle – they need a super-sub. Fortunately, God is a good manager and he had Jesus ready on the side line to step in and save the team called the human race. Jesus willingly ran onto the field, was born of a virgin in an animal stable, played a 'blinder' (was without sin), and then brought a great victory, but had to die in our place as part of the process. Jesus is our substitute. The guiltless one became guilty on our behalf. This is not what we actually deserve, nor is this anything we could accomplish by our own means. Our only option is to willingly, joyfully, humbly and graciously accept this free gift. What a salvation, what a substitute!

In another example, a court judge declares someone as guilty but then steps down into the dock to take the set punishment on their behalf, cancelling all the obligations of the debtor.[13]

Selah.

---

[13] Berkhof, L. *Systematic Theology*, P378.

Propitiation

This word does need a bit more investigation to better grasp it. Propitiation simply means to appease someone who has been offended. Punishment is appeased by the removal of sin, and this enables reconciliation to take place.[14]

Starting with offence. God is unable, I believe, to be offended in the same way we are because that might indicate a weakness in his personhood or perhaps a chink in his divine nature. He does know all things ahead of time too, so he would have no need for that. However, propitiation is an action that appeases a lowercase 'g' god, spirit, or person – all of whom can and do easily get upset and take offence. Let's be honest, we all tend to do that more often than we would like to admit. If we look a little further though, offence does not only mean getting upset or even an attacking sports team, it can also mean a breach of a law or rule, so an illegal act. Now we are getting somewhere. God is holy and going against his ways is sin. We sin and God does not like it but he does not throw a tantrum, he remains a Holy God unable himself to sin. But he does need a way to deal with the issue, however.

Now to appease. This is the act of gaining or regaining the favour or goodwill of someone, to satisfy, allay, or relieve them. Allay means to diminish or put to rest. So, to put to rest God's issue with sin and gain his grace over it and forgiveness of it, he must be appeased.

---

[14] Thiessen. H. C. *Lectures in Systematic Theology* (Grand Rapids: William B. Eerdmans Publishing Company, 1979), P238-9.

When we use the term propitiation or realistically something similar like, 'God's wrath against sin has been satisfied', we mean that God's issue with sin has been put to rest against those who have sinned against him. God's rightful wrath against sin is appeased and we receive his love and mercy instead. How is this achieved? Simple. Jesus! He died as a one-time blood sacrifice to deal with the issue of sin and to prevent humanity from experiencing ongoing separation from God, which is the worst kind of poverty. With our guilt and shame removed by Jesus, we are rescued from this eternal separation from God and we no longer need to fear him or his wrath, instead we... *"approach God's throne of grace with confidence, so that we may receive mercy and find grace to help us in our time of need"* (Heb. 4:16).

Isn't it amazingly paradoxical that God would send a part of the Godhead or Trinity, to fix his issue with sin? He sacrificed perfection for our imperfection. This is another absolutely incredible part of our salvation. I think God is more committed to helping us than we could ever imagine.

Selah.

Justification

Because God is a just God, he could not free anyone from their sin until his own demand for justice had been satisfied.[15] He achieved this by crediting to all those who accept Jesus, the

---

[15] Thiessen. H. C. *Lectures in Systematic Theology*, P237.

perfect righteousness of Jesus.[16] Therefore, it is only possible to be justified in God's eyes through faith in Jesus (Rom. 1:17). *Justificatio sola fide* is the Latin, and this doctrine affirms that it is only through faith that we are saved and not through doing good works. Although good works for Jesus and his Kingdom should naturally follow. It is through Jesus, that God justifies the actions of the ungodly, that's you and me, and remarkably we become guiltless, made right, or at peace with God as our relationship with him is restored as it was originally intended.

Justification and righteousness come from the same root word *dikai*. In his letters to the Roman and Galatian believers, Paul has an almost exclusive use of this word. Justify, *dikaioo*, is used fourteen times and righteousness, *dikaiosune*, fifty-two times.[17]

This concept would have been unthinkable and completely stunned the Jewish culture at the time of Jesus, who understood the consequences of breaking the laws of Moses in the OT. This meant guilt, judgment, punishment and condemnation. But in the NT, our righteousness as disciples of Jesus now surpasses that of the religious leaders, the Pharisees, and as his people we are acquitted. Jesus' complete and perfect righteousness is imputed or ascribed or placed upon us as a free gift, so it is not something we can own, possess or claim that we in any way achieved. All glory to Jesus.

---

[16] Milne, B. *Know The Truth. A Handbook of Christian Belief* (Leicester: Inter-Varsity Press, 1982), P188.

[17] Ladd, G. E. *A Theology of the New Testament*, P428.

God declares us as righteous or having right standing before him, even though we are not yet perfected and we do still sin – hopefully by ever-decreasing measure. We are now viewed this way because of Jesus' sacrifice on the cross and are innocent by implication because we now belong to Jesus.

Black helpfully contributes that justification means we are declared righteous and therefore not condemned, a legal declaration in which we are not 'made' righteous – we still get things wrong – but gain a new status: Christ's righteousness is given to us.[18] It is immediate and does not require we work towards it, coming by faith alone, *sola fide*.[19] We are not justified by good works and therefore we do not keep our justification by them either. The works we do flow from our faith and demonstrate our declared righteousness.[20]

There will be a final judgment day and all our sins, past, present and future, are covered. God will also vindicate us for when we have been wronged, so we don't need to seek revenge. This incredible position that we now hold should lead us into loving obedience and living holy lives, both with and for the Holy God who saved us. As mentioned earlier, it is not a licence to behave as we like or continue in sin.

Selah.

---

[18] Black, J. *Apostolic Theology. A Trinitarian Evangelical Pentecostal Introduction to Christian Doctrine* (Luton: The Apostolic Church, 2016), P395-7.

[19] Ibid, P407.

[20] Ibid, P411-13.

Redemption

If we redeem something it means that we buy it back. In this process, ownership of the item changes. Examples might be to redeem a mortgage on a house so that the lending bank no longer has an interest or investment in your property; to regain possession of an item that had to temporarily be pawned; to pay off a car loan; or in an extreme situation to pay a kidnapper a ransom to have your loved one returned. In all of these cases, a full and final payment always has to be made. If this is not the case then ownership does not change and the items could be taken from you, lost, or never returned. When we think of people and salvation, the word redemption means to be saved from the consequences of sin and the payment of debt, or perhaps the release of a captive.[21] Before choosing to become disciples of Jesus, that was exactly our predicament and situation. We were slaves to sin with no way of making that final payment and to be released from its penalty. Very thankfully though... "*in him [Jesus] we have redemption through his blood*" (Eph. 1:7).

Our redemption from sin, our release, was so very costly. It cost Jesus his life, through an agonising death, and his being separated from his Father as he bore the sins of this world. This heavenly transaction that is salvation, changes our ownership. We leave the kingdom of darkness and enter the Kingdom of Heaven. Instead of our own poor and weak ownership of ourselves, we now come under the greatest possible King and the most wonderful owner – Jesus. The Father and Son are one,

---

[21] Thiessen. H. C. *Lectures in Systematic Theology*, P240.

and so yes, when we belong to Christ we also belong to the Father as well, we are adopted into his family... "*God sent his Son, born of a woman, born under the law, to **redeem** those under the law, that we might receive **adoption to sonship**. Because you are his sons, **God sent the Spirit of his Son into our hearts**, the Spirit who calls out, "Abba, Father." **So you are no longer a slave, but God's child**; and since you are his child, God has made you also an heir*" (Gal. 4:4b-7). What an incredible Trinitarian scripture that is. Father, Son and Holy Spirit were all involved in your salvation, with Jesus making it possible through his sacrifice for you to enter into the Kingdom of Heaven. We were like perpetual slaves with no way of gaining our own freedom, and we have simply and suddenly been freed or emancipated. Jesus paid the price that we simply could not pay. Now that we have been freed from slavery to sin, we willingly become obedient disciples. We are the redeemed.

Selah.

Reconciliation

We now reach our seventh and final word that helps us to better comprehend our rescue. We do certainly know that the original relationship God designed for himself and humanity was good. It was mankind who broke the trust and freedom they had been given, damaging the relationship to the point of separation. Now that humanity, when born into this world, is estranged from God, we need to be reconciled to him. God can do just fine on his own and he is fully able and sufficient without us – he does not need us in the way that we need him. In his grace and mercy though, God does not only reconcile us so that we might be polite to one another again, but he fully restores the relationship and our past sins are no longer held against us. This was part of God's plan: knowing as he did that the separation would take place, he initiated a way for complete restoration, through the work of his Son on the cross... "*while we were God's enemies, **we were reconciled to him through the death of his Son**, how much more, having been reconciled, shall we be **saved through his life!** Not only is this so, but we also boast in God through our Lord Jesus Christ, through whom **we have now received reconciliation**"* (Rom. 5:10-11). God's love initiated reconciliation and Jesus' love accomplished it, by removing the impenetrable barrier of sin.

As we have already seen, because of Jesus, the writer to the Hebrew believers, tells us that we can indeed boldly approach his throne. We are not approaching an ornate chair, but rather the very God of this universe who sits on it. The relationship is restored fully and we are reconciled. The Bible says that we even become friends with God once more... "*I have called you friends, for everything that I learned from my Father I have made known to you*" (John 15:15). I don't mean these things in an irreverent way, but somehow, they are true. We could never have achieved this ourselves and so God, in his amazing providence, foresaw that – how wonderful!

The Greek word for reconciliation, *katallasso*, comes from *kata* meaning an exact point, which brings an intensity to *allasso*, meaning to change or exchange. Therefore, a proper and decisive change does take place at the point in time when we move from enmity to harmony with God.

Perhaps the clearest example of reconciliation is the parable of the Prodigal Son (Luke 15:11-32). The son has everything he could need: good relationship with his father and access to the family's land, cattle and wealth. Yet the son chooses to go his own way, takes off and squanders his prematurely taken inheritance. Soon destitute and with no food, the son returns to his father, hoping to become one of his workers as he remembers that they at least had enough food to eat. The son represents fallen humanity. The father's response when he sees his son returning home is one of great joy, and an immediate and full restoration takes place with him granting the son all the privileges that his sonship entailed. The father represents God. This is the underserved reconciliation that we gain.

Yes, we are reconciled to God the Father, through Jesus the sacrificial Son when we are saved. This benefit is for us to enjoy, but also for us to go and share with others... *"this is from God, who reconciled us to himself through Christ and gave us the ministry of reconciliation"* (2 Cor. 5:18). We certainly receive reconciliation but for another purpose too. We gain so very much, but we are then also to become ministers of this grace to others, to tell them about what we received and to facilitate their opportunity to likewise receive. Salvation means that our relationship and fellowship with God is once again enabled. Peace with God, and therefore true inner peace, ensues, and remarkably we get to share this so that others too can make their peace with God.[22]

Selah.

---

[22] Ladd, G. E. *A Theology of the New Testament*, P456.

In Conclusion

We have seen the incredible ways in which we are changed when we are 'saved', and what we have now become because of Jesus. We looked at the meaning of seven words and their concepts: atonement, vicarious, substitutionary, propitiation, redemption, justification and ending with reconciliation. What an incredible blessing salvation is, as relationship with God is made possible only in the completed work of Jesus. Without his historical, literal and bodily resurrection there would be no salvation, no eternal life and no Christianity.[23] I pray that you have been wowed once again by your rescue. Go out this week and rescue someone else!

---

[23] Warrington, K. *Pentecostal Theology*, P35.

CHAPTER THREE

Living Out Your Salvation

It's Supposed to Make a Difference

In just seven words our world gets turned upside down: atonement, vicarious, substitutionary, propitiation, and also justification, redemption and reconciliation. There are others too, but my point is...can knowing all of this, alongside being able to experience God personally, have no impact upon us? Of course it can, if it is just head knowledge, and unfortunately many so-called disciples of Jesus live this only as a piece of academic knowledge, without allowing it to penetrate their whole being and behaviour accordingly.

However, if there is a **true heartfelt realisation** and a **Spirit-led revelation** of what it means to be saved, then surely not. Yet even with this, life will at times still require us to 'hang on by our finger tips' to our faith. We are not promised a smooth ride in this life when we follow Jesus. We do though sometimes seem to forget the marvel and the wonder of what happened to us when we were saved. Hopefully, it will not be like this too often in our journeying with Jesus, as there will also be wonderful mountain top experiences and encounters with our King. If we decide, purposefully or subconsciously, not to be fully committed to being this new person or creation that we have become, with a constant willingness to change, then we can end up sitting back again with 'cruise control' switched on, and simply going through the motions.

Our salvation is not just a legal condition but rather it is a truly authentic and a vital reality. After salvation and all the glorious things that take place, we committed ourselves to continually choose to make Jesus our Lord. We allow him full access to our hearts so that he can implement his ways within us, because they are far above our ways. Jesus does this as he interacts with us relationally and personally, through the Word – the *logos* written word (the Bible) and the *rhema* spoken word (by the Holy Spirit). We are not supposed only to learn the 'rules of the game' but we are also then meant to play! We do so by applying his ways to our lives and how we live, not by just knowing what they are. It is not played out through a social or a 'support your community' type ethic with Jesus kept in isolation. No, in all that we do, whether church focused or community focused, Jesus must be present with our reliance remaining firmly in him as we go.

Those who profess faith in Jesus are still able, if they wish, to behave more like the dominion of the other kingdoms around them. Just look at the moral failings found in believers of Jesus. The divorce rate is the same in the Church of Jesus as it is in the worldly kingdoms. Look at abusive Christian leaders and pastors – need I say more. What this inconsistent behaviour does though, is make Christians and therefore the Church look hypocritical and weak, shedding a poor light on who Jesus is and often making little real impact on the lives of the people we know, or into the wider societal culture around us. Essentially, living as far less effective citizens. Why do we allow sin to still have mastery over us? Often, we are in the Kingdom of Heaven but simply don't live like it. The world, or those belonging to other kingdoms, can spot hypocrisy a mile off.

They do so very easily indeed. Our role is to overcome the kingdoms of this world, through the undefeatable Kingdom of Heaven, by participating in it and by consistently modelling Jesus' holy lifestyle to others.[24]

My prayer is, either for the first time or by way of reminder, that **a fresh realisation of how incredible salvation is will motivate you to change, to run back to Jesus and fall in love with him all over again**. Perhaps this will mean picking yourself up once more or continuing in your advancement with and in him. Have you been wowed once more? After all, it is supposed to make a difference. Refocusing on your salvation does have the power to change you if you will only let it. This inward change should also affect your outward behaviour... *"A good man brings good things out of the good stored up in his heart, and an evil man brings evil things out of the evil stored up in his heart. For the mouth speaks what the heart is full of"* (Luke 6:45). The question is – do you still need a 'heart' transplant?

We do seek forgiveness, with repentance from the heart, to enable the salvation transaction to take place, but as soon as that is done, the primary thing for a new-born disciple of Jesus is to now seek the Kingdom above everything else, actively walking with and learning from Jesus. In seeking him we learn to hear him, to trust him, to obey him, to have faith and confidence in him. While this is an ongoing learning and growing process, it is not meant to be an intellectual assent to

[24] Willard, D., Black, G. *The Divine Conspiracy Continued. Fulfilling God's Kingdom on Earth* (London: William Collins, 2014), P307.

knowledge in some form of isolation from day-to-day living. Jesus didn't only come for our salvation but also to bring us new life (John 10:10; 1 John 5:11-12). This life does not promise happiness and smooth sailing or financial prosperity just because we have been saved and joined the Kingdom. Instead, it promises a close walk with Jesus during both the good and the very trying times in life. Discipleship bridges the gap between a salvific prayer and an ongoing transformation of our character. **We are to continue being transformed inwardly by revelation and the teachings of Jesus, which we then outwardly demonstrate to others**. Jesus is alive and wanting to walk this journey with you. Will you join your life totally with his?

Compartmentalised Christianity

We can often live a compartmentalised form of Christianity, doing church on Sundays and even attending a mid-week group, but only behaving like Christians at those gatherings. As soon as we are at home or the office or down at the golf or football club, we move into a different form of behaviour i.e. the common behaviour of that particular place. My own life was like this as a young Christian. This led to me not always seeming very different to other people who did not know Jesus, all because I sought their acceptance. If you are still doing this, no matter how many years you have been a Christian, then I urge you to stop, to re-prioritise seeking first the Kingdom, and to live as a true citizen of the Kingdom. Stop wasting time being ineffective, with one foot in and one foot out.

It's an Apprenticeship

I left school at the age of sixteen and became an apprentice engineer. I have fond memories of the company I worked at, Martin-Baker Aircraft Company[25]. In this role, I had to learn discipline and the repetition of things to become skilled at them. I had many experienced teachers, some of who had worked there for more than forty years! They would take time to demonstrate a task or skill and then watch as I tried the same, guiding and correcting me along the way until I could do it with skill and unaided. I moved from department to department in order to become skilled in multiple areas of engineering and eventually to become qualified. This was a four-year process.

Every apprentice has to be with their teacher, and it takes time to gain skills from them. The same is true of Jesus: to be his apprentice you have to be with him and learn how to be like him. While he is not here on planet earth physically, he is here spiritually through the Holy Spirit, through his word and through other believers who have grown to become disciple-makers. For believers to choose to be real apprentices of Jesus, after they are saved, they have to change their belief system about discipleship and the Kingdom as being of primary importance for their faith, so that they will want to do so enthusiastically. This is vital because it is a tough journey at times, but it is the most wonderful adventure a person can go on. If we fail to do so, then the true significance and power of the Kingdom will not be realised in us, or through us and into

---

[25] www.martin-baker.com

this world. We will only see an ever-expanding consumer type of Christianity.

Disciples will learn many skills like how to proclaim the gospel message of the Kingdom and its King. Not all of us will have teacher as our primary five-fold ministry gifting (Eph. 4:11-13) but we can and must all teach what we know. We should be becoming multi-skilled in these areas of ministry and doing so in our weaker areas will make us more rounded and able. Disciples should also learn how to manifest or demonstrate the Kingdom of Heaven because it is a Kingdom of power not just of words (1 Cor. 4:20). Encountering Jesus through the Holy Spirit is necessary for us to be able to demonstrate his power to others. Disciples must learn to teach others what they have learned themselves through practice (2 Tim. 2:2), but this is not merely an educational equipping but a real and hands-on apprenticeship style of learning. Perhaps we spend too much time in church 'meetings' and while these are wonderful and necessary, they are for the purpose of sending us out to make a difference in our sphere of influence. They are a starting point and a place of refreshing and releasing, not the end destination.

In Conclusion

Although life can be tough at times, God does mean for those situations ultimately to be for our good. If we are closet Christians, then it's time to come out and to stop living our lives in different compartments. It is now time to embrace an apprenticeship style of journeying with and learning from Jesus, as well as from other believers.

Knowing all of this should lead to a yielded willingness that allows God to transform our very character, to be like his Son Jesus, and make a **real heartfelt difference** as we assimilate this great work into **our daily living,**[26] as citizens of the Kingdom. Perhaps this could all be summed up in a single word: **gratefulness**.

---

[26] Berkhof, L. *Systematic Theology*, P415.

CHAPTER FOUR

The Importance of Authenticity

I thought that at the beginning of a chapter on authenticity it would be helpful to have some form of definition of what I think an authentic disciple of Jesus actually is. There are many such definitions and you are free to follow whichever one helps you to best understand your walk of faith with Jesus. For me, a disciple is someone who...**knows and obeys the Father** (Matt. 7:21; 12:50), **lives increasingly like Jesus** (2 Cor. 3:18), **walks in the power of the Holy Spirit** (Gal. 5:25), **and teaches others what they have learned** (Matt. 28:20; 2 Tim. 2:2).[27]

We all have to be able to hear God's voice. In the OT Book of Habakkuk (2:1-2) and the NT Book of Revelation (1:10-11) we see that we can learn this through becoming still, listening for God's spontaneous thoughts, looking for pictures or visions (moving pictures or scenes), and writing them down. This will help us to better distinguish between our thoughts, those from the enemy and those that are from God. Then we need to obey what God is asking of us.

We are to become like Jesus in every way as we have already seen in chapter one.

---

[27] Thank you, my friend Pastor Rafael Gutiérrez, for discipling me in this small but helpful way and to understand this concept.

We are to walk in the power of the Holy Spirit, which will be discussed later in section two.

We are all disciples of someone, perhaps through what our surrounding culture tries to tell us or some form of educational programme. Therefore, we all learn and continue to learn from others. It is critically important to learn from Jesus and other disciples of his, so that we can do what he did, and then teach others what we have learnt.[28]

A Cause to Live For

Humanity needs a cause to live for, and if necessary, to die for. Jesus and his Kingdom is that very thing. Keeping an eternal and heavenly Kingdom Perspective will help us to do just that. Following Jesus with the whole being will bring life's greatest adventure as well as its toughest challenges. It is the utmost privilege to know God personally. It is in this relationship that Christ lives in us (Col. 1:27) and he is also formed in us (Gal. 4:19; 2 Cor. 3:18) by the regenerating and transformational work of the Holy Spirit. Realising that the power of God is in us is just incredible, but also being enabled to demonstrate it is wonderfully mind-blowing.

The cause of Christ continues through us as his disciples today, and we do therefore have the greatest cause to live for. His mission has become our mission: the extension of the influence of his great Kingdom into the lives of those who do not yet know him. We get to do this by being a willing disciple, but also

[28] Willard, D. *The Divine Conspiracy. Rediscovering Our Hidden Life in God* (London: William Collins, 1998), P297.

by then helping to make other disciples. Jesus revolutionises us from the inside out, in proportion to our ongoing willingness to allow him the full access to our hearts that he desires. The more like him we become, the more effective we will be for him and his mission.

Sadly, much of the church could be described as weak, because it is not fully committed to the cause of the Kingdom or willing to give every part of themselves to Jesus. Therefore, low level of spiritual life and formation often prevails, even in church leaders. We have to recognise and allow the Holy Spirit to bring us this greater spiritual formation and deal with the areas of the soul that are not yet completely made whole. We all have been wounded by life's circumstances and by people, and it is often out of a lack of inner healing that we react poorly, which then leads us to further extend, sometimes unwittingly, our hurts to others.

The Church often has as its main goal getting people into heaven, rather than getting heaven into people. The latter can be harder to do and generally is not the main goal of the Church. But that is what Jesus tasked us to do – to go and make disciples. **We must focus on making disciples if we hope to be effective in continuing the mission of Jesus**.

Authentic Christian Living

In the era that Jesus walked this earth with his first generation of disciples, the Hebrew or Jewish culture in which they lived and ministered had a close match between their thinking and how that impacted their daily living. In contrast, both their former Greek and then-current Roman occupation cultures were much more philosophical, with a wide gap between their theories of life and how they actually lived. So, what kind of culture do you live in today? Is it more Jewish, that had one God, more Greek or Roman, that had many gods, or is it other and secular i.e. with no gods? Are our values and our beliefs worlds apart from how we live? Are they mere philosophies? Jesus lived the most authentic life of anyone, with his words and actions working in beautiful harmony, and with not a hint of hypocrisy. We as his disciples today need to be authentic, we need to get real. I can remember a famous UK 1970's band call 'The Real Thing' and their most well-known song "Can you feel the force". They weren't! Can you remember the Coke-a-cola adverts in which they claimed that their drink was the real thing? It isn't! So, what does it mean to be real, to be an authentic disciple?

The word authentic means something of undisputed origin supported by unquestionable evidence, something that is genuine and verified, something that is not false or copied, something real and true, something reliable and trustworthy.

I think it is worth expanding these concepts a little, by way of some challenging questions...

Something of undisputed origin, supported by unquestionable evidence. Is your salvation and ongoing walk with Jesus undisputed by all who know you, and could you or others provide unquestionable evidence to support this as fact? Would a judge and jury find you innocent in a court of law if you made this claim as a disciple?

Something genuine and verified. Specialists are often used to determine if valuable items are genuine or fake, like an old oil painting or a piece made by a master craftsman. How genuine are you?

Something that is not false or copied. Are you always honest and uniquely you, never trying to be someone else? Like Levi's 501 Jeans – are you your own 'the original' thing; perhaps like an original and legal document or a passport?

Something real and true Do you exist as a living and active disciple who is always truthful – including to yourself and to your testimony of faith?

Something reliable and trustworthy. Is your 'yes' a yes and your 'no' a no? In other words, do you mean what you say and do you carry it out, and are you consistent?

My favourite synonym of authentic is proper or 'pukka'. In my homeland of England, we have a brand of savoury pie called "Pukka Pies", and they are genuinely awesome pies! Are you a pukka disciple of Jesus?

If someone is authentic, they accurately and properly represent their true nature or beliefs. Do you accurately and properly represent the nature of Jesus? If you describe something as authentic, you mean that it is almost the same as, or as good as, the original. Are you almost the same as Jesus?

I am as challenged by all of this as you might be. I know it wasn't a test, but how would you honestly score yourself? I hope that living as an authentic Christian hasn't shocked you too much so far, because there is more...

Authentic in Purpose

The Church (and any Christian ministry or organisation) is supposed to exist to represent and extend the influence of the Kingdom of Heaven here on earth. The ways and means in which that takes place may well vary in each local church context and setting (often referred to as its mission), but I wonder if all churches are aiming at the same thing. Is the church remaining authentic to its purpose? Regardless of which church you are a part of, or how well it is doing in this regard, you can still live with this as the main purpose for your own life. This is your purpose in life: **to know your King and to extend the influence of his Kingdom**. Whatever words we prefer to use to describe this, that is essentially why we exist. Are you as a disciple being authentic to your purpose and to your particular calling and way of achieving this?

Authentic in Mission

How does your local church (ministry or organisation) choose to authentically live out the wider purpose of Jesus' ministry? For my church, we use the tagline or mission statement 'Discipleship for Mission'. We have our local reason to exist, which may well be different from other local churches because we are not all meant to be carbon copies of each other. A friend of mine uses 'Saved to Serve' for his church. Their focus is serving, whilst ours is to make disciples who see themselves as missionaries. In both of these cases, the method might be different, but the wider purpose is intended and not lost. Both can help to build people with a commitment to live in purity, portraying the character of Jesus in their midst and to the world around us. That means locally and further afield too. Mission gives us the 'why' we exist and is the filter through which everything else is passed. This is because we desire to make disciples of Jesus and release them into their calling and destiny. Perhaps you have never thought of mission and how that might apply directly to you as a disciple of Jesus. I hope this has got you thinking and praying.

Authentic in Vision

Without vision we know that people perish, let go of hope or even go their own way... "*Where there is no vision, the people perish*" (Prov. 29:18). So how can we be authentic in vision? Vision gives us the 'what' that we are aiming at or our direction of travel. Vision brings excitement, enthusiasm and energy as well as hope, and facilitates lives that are lived on an adventure with Jesus. Everyone develops by finding ways to get behind and involved in the vision of their church or group, as they function in their individual calling. What is it that you would you like to achieve in your walk with God, where he has placed you?

Authentic in Relationship with God

We need to keep asking God to give us the Spirit of wisdom and revelation in order for us to know him better (Eph. 1:17). I believe that in doing this we are to encounter Father, Son and Holy Spirit. Being authentic in our encountering God means connecting with him in the ways that we would most naturally. Perhaps for you that is reading the Bible, or praying, or singing, or dancing, or painting, or prophesying, or walking in nature. Use those ways in which he has wired you to best connect with him. But at the same time, I would urge you for your own growth to try other ways to also connect with him that are not quite so comfortable. This will give you a greater appreciation of those who might connect with, or worship, God in a slightly different way than which you might personally prefer. I might not be comfortable myself dancing around the church, but I can choose not to judge and instead to enjoy watching others doing so, and on occasion it is also good for me to 'throw caution to the wind' and just dance like King David did (2 Sam. 6:14).

We are the temple, that is being built upon a foundation of authentic worship and a partnering of intercession with the Holy Spirit. We are raising an army that recognises who the real enemy is and stands together to defeat his strategies. This all takes a sacrifice of our time, but it should be joyous because in God's presence we find authentic and lasting joy. This is why we worship and why we petition God to be present in all that we do. Joy is found in the very essence of God's character... "*strength and joy fill his dwelling*" (1 Chron 16:27). We do this to hear and experience God and also to discover who we are in him. This is so that we can live our lives out of the worth and value that he places on each one of us individually. Let us, therefore, be authentic in our relationship with our heavenly Father, his Son Jesus, and the incredible Holy Spirit.

Authentic in Growth

God has placed us, even in smaller settings, into a diverse community. That is because we are all different and unique even if we all happen to be from a very similar background, gender, race and culture. Add to that, the different views on theological topics and we have a mishmash of people 'thrown together' by God who are then expected to live in unity and harmony with each other.

With all these differences, God will use them to grow us and to shape us, if we remain willing to learn. Even the greatest of church leaders can and should be continuing to learn from God, through his word and the people he has placed around them. We must continue to develop as disciples. This authentic equipping will not always be plain sailing but it will deepen our intimacy with God, our understanding of the scriptures and our heartfelt love for others.

I do love God's written word and I recently preached on Psalm 119, which reminds us of our commitment to it. The Bible is so very necessary for us to grow in understanding and also in fresh revelation of God as these ancient words come alive in our hearts today. I believe this is an essential area of growth. However, this should not become merely an academic exercise, divorced from the relational connection with God. It is through its practical application to daily living that we grow spiritually. For example, we learn about spiritual gifts from the Bible and how they are to be used and then we learn to use them personally through practice. This grows us spiritually and at the same time affects others, as we become used in the process of God giving his gifts through us, like healing. The use of spiritual gifts is how we demonstrate the power of the Kingdom and they help to release us into our calling and become a church that is able to minister them with confidence to others. Discipleship means growing in both Word and Spirit. The challenge is to identify personal calling and gifting, and to grow in these, whilst simultaneously serving the vision of the church or group that God has placed us in. This in turn, increases our churches ability to reach out to our wider local community, creating a win-win-win.

Authentic in Sharing

Disciples make up a worldwide family that has a passionate commitment to the mission of God, sharing the good news of Jesus in word, in speech and in loving action. This is simply known as evangelism. I realise that we might not all be natural evangelists, but I do believe that we are all called to evangelise. No matter the style we find most comfortable, it is Jesus' love that compels us to do so (2 Cor. 5:14). We attempt to reconcile to God people that do not know him, because we no longer live for ourselves but him. Perhaps we prefer to help paint a neighbour's fence and get a chance to share why we would do such a thing. We need to build relationships and journey with people giving them the opportunity to see and follow Jesus for themselves. If we prefer to pray for healing for random people on the streets, then their healing can be a more noticeable demonstration of the Kingdom. Either way, both can afford us those opportunities to speak to people about Jesus. This is evangelism.

Again, if we would on occasion attempt other methods that are not in our comfort zones, then we will grow. This is why short-term mission is so vital. In preparation for mission, we are able to prepare ourselves for any eventuality, and for any opportunity that presents itself. We commit ourselves to being Jesus' hands and feet for the mission's duration. This can of course be in our local area, not only to the farther reaches of this world. However, overseas mission is important to be able to grow in sharing sensitively outside one's usual cultural context. In this, we will grow further as we share Jesus. We go with a 'Kingdom first' mentality and this type of heart attitude, with our own church second. If we bring unity by supporting other churches and ministries, I believe that God will not leave our church or group out, as he extends the influence of his Kingdom through each.

Authentic in Relationships with others

The people who make up our church, including ourselves, may often be great at 'surface level'. "How are you doing? Oh, I'm doing just fine thanks". Then we talk about the weather, or is that only those of us in England? Being authentic in all of our relationships necessitates that we learn to go deeper than the surface level. Why is this harder to do? I would say it is because we have to make ourselves vulnerable in the process. To share what is going on in our struggles and to listen, without judging, to the struggles of others.

In the church I lead, we create the opportunity for triplets, of the same gender, to join together each month to go deeper, to practise being authentic. This is perhaps one of the most important areas we have and at the same time is the most difficult to achieve. The proof is in the lower level of attendance when compared to other areas. It takes time, to build authentic relationships and engage openly and honestly with each other. We need to move away from a mentality of staying hidden because we think others may not like the real me, to one that wants to find freedom, learn and offer their part in the authentic discipling of others. Instead, we would rather look the part outwardly even though our inner person might well be in a critical condition... *"These people come near to me with their mouth and honour me with their lips, but their hearts are far from me"* (Isa. 29:13). We can be authentic and yet at the same time flawed. We 'expose' our inner condition to get help from God and others. He, and they, will still love us.

I'm guessing most of you would know and like, the scripture that says... *"the prayer of a righteous person is powerful and effective"*, from the Book of James. I think we would all like our prayers to be both powerful and effective. If we read the part just before this, then we see it in its fuller and proper context... *"the prayer offered in faith will make the sick person well; the Lord will raise them up. If they have sinned, they will be forgiven. Therefore* **confess your sins to each other and pray for each other so that you may be healed**. *The prayer of a righteous person is powerful and effective"* (James 5:15-16). If you are in trouble or struggling or sick or have sinned, then sharing and praying through these is the context in which your prayers will be both powerful and effective. But how often do we allow ourselves firstly, even to be in this type of setting and secondly, to be vulnerable enough in them to create trust and authentic relationship?

Healing can be: physical, emotional, mental and spiritual. So, confessing or sharing how we are doing with others remains important for us to ensure we are authentic in our discipleship, and to allow God's healing touch into every area of our being, as well as into those that we are wanting to help. That is why we need to have one or two trusted folks pray with us and over us, as we do for them. When we are healed or made whole then we can be more effective for the Kingdom.

It is in these authentic relationships, which have gone deeper, that other people who have not yet committed their lives to be a disciple of Jesus, take note. They stand out, a bit like a 'sore thumb', but in a good way. They see deeply loving, trusting and caring relationships that the world around them, without Jesus, simply cannot match. These relationships impact not only the lives of people in them, who need that love and care, but everyone else who is watching (John 13:35). What a wonderful witness of Jesus it is when we care this deeply for each other. Just imagine your whole church gathering full of these types of relationships. Everyone will benefit. This will take a real and determined commitment from every disciple to do life with one another. It is difficult, but it's where you make disciples. The enemy does not want us free and will do whatever he can to prevent an open, honest, and authentic discipleship journey. He does not want us to be effective or to obey Jesus' command to go and make disciples. But knowing this – we do have the upper hand.

Even as a pastor, I choose to commit to friendships and people that I can share my personal life with and also listen to and help. Being authentic in relationships has warranted at times an appropriate sharing with my wider congregation. In being real, I can and do share my victories and testimonies, and on occasion things like the spiritual weight I carry. This includes practical and financial responsibilities, stress, feelings of loneliness, or even the effects of sometimes seeing sporadic or waning commitment from others, or people always wanting things their way. It is not plain sailing all of the time.

Now, your church may do things in very different ways, and that is totally fine, as long as authentic relationships are being encouraged, and it continues to be a home that genuinely welcomes all who enter its doors as if they were already family.

Authentic in Discipleship Making

As Christians, we often like to be well fed ourselves, which is completely natural and normal as we wish to grow in our journey of faith, and to reach the destiny that God has for our lives. Like in the natural or physical realm, it is not good when we don't eat, and likewise, when we stop participating in our faith, we become weak and spiritually malnourished. We must have a balanced diet, a spiritual intake to help us to grow well, or mature, building a strong root system beneath us. While life can and does throw difficult situations at us, they help us in this maturing process and we often grow more in harder times than when all is going well. Because we may find times of struggle almost overwhelming, we can tend just to 'hang on in there'. Growing as a disciple is difficult enough. However, this can often leave us in a perpetual state of feeding ourselves and just coping, when we are supposed to go beyond ourselves and to make disciples of others. All disciples can do this. I do understand that less mature disciples will likely need more discipling than those more mature, but not always, and the more mature can still learn from the less mature. As adults, we find out that we can still learn great lessons in this life from our children and grandchildren, who even unknowingly continue to teach us things.

How do we make disciples? Well, we teach them... "*to obey everything I have commanded you. And surely I am with you always, to the very end of the age*" (Matt. 28:20). What happens though, if we don't have the ministry or giftings of a teacher? I don't believe that this excludes anyone. Like with evangelism, we may not be an evangelist but we must all evangelise; here too we may not all be gifted teachers but we must teach. We teach all the time, just not in an academic setting. We teach children to ride a bicycle or a pensioner how to use modern technology, for example. As disciples, we are to teach others to obey his commands or his laws. We have to know what they are and be willing to share what we have learnt with others. God's loving and helpful laws, must be something we can all teach. We know where they are (Matt 5, 6, 7) and we also know that if we practise them and teach them, we will be great in the Kingdom (Matt. 5:19). How often are you teaching others about...anger, purity, biblical marriage, honesty, not taking revenge and not hating but instead loving? These are just the six laws of how to love your neighbour. I wonder if these are topics that we ever think about, discuss or help teach others. Who are you teaching the commands that God has given us, in his laws of the Kingdom? **This is a Kingdom of words!**

If we, as disciples, are expected to demonstrate the power of the Kingdom, then which gifts of the Spirit are we functioning in, or are being used through us, to bless others? Paul, in writing to the Corinthian church, wants the disciples there to be both informed and authentic in their use of spiritual gifts. He wants them to have a measure against which they can judge what is authentic and he provides two: 1) when speaking by the Spirit people cannot say "*Jesus be cursed*" and, 2) only by the Spirit can people say *"Jesus is Lord"* (1 Cor. 12:1-3). The Holy Spirit, working through disciples, bears witness to the lordship of Christ, and significantly, the Spirit lives in us to help us as we endure this journey that we call life. Paul gives us this helpful and beneficial test of authenticity in these matters. **This is a Kingdom of power!**

In Conclusion

We have the greatest possible cause to live for and so our words and actions need to match closely with what we believe. Jesus is our King and he is calling us to a life of excellence, knowing that this will require a full commitment from us. Are we the real thing, the real deal – are we authentic? I hope that we now see how important this is.

Are we authentic in all of these ways – in our purpose, our mission, our vision, in our relationship with God, in our growth, in our sharing, in our relationships with others and in making disciples? Authentic discipleship is costly. If you want to be an Olympic champion you have to dedicate your life to your sport – you have to be 'all in'. It's the same with authentic discipleship. **Your salvation was free, but true discipleship will cost you everything that you are and everything that you have**. If that statement causes you to 'take a breath' or to 'pause for thought', then let me encourage you – it will be very much worth it. You will grow and therefore benefit, and so will those closest to you. A better version of you awaits, one that is released to be all that God intended you to be.

Now try and imagine your whole church or group gathering being a place where all are on this same journey into being an authentic disciple, becoming a body that serves with a joy that cannot be quenched and humility that cannot be faked. Not yet perfect, but that is a people full of love for one another, so much so, that the world around will sit up and take notice.

In Summary

As we end this first section, I hope that you have been inspired by what Jesus achieved for you by way of his rescue plan, that you have learnt or been reminded again how great your salvation really is and the lengths God has gone to provide it, and that you realise it is to be lived out in your everyday life. I want to encourage you to be as authentic a citizen as you possibly can.

Perhaps you have been challenged in this foundational offering of what a real disciple is, but this is vital to grasp before we move onto section two. Because next, we will journey a little deeper into what predominately Matthew's Gospel shows us, about the making of a disciple!

The Making of a Disciple

CHAPTER ONE

Citizens Are Convinced

Whenever we attempt to bring change or something new, there will often be resistance. It could be a simple change of format in church services or a change of procedure in your office, some will push back as they do not like change and prefer things just as they are. Stability is cherished. As citizens of the Kingdom, we know that we are to love **God** above everything else (Matt. 22:37) and to love our **neighbour** as **ourselves** (Matt. 22:39). These things, if we do them, will bring stability to our lives – like the legs of a three-legged stool to sit on. This type of stability is good and positive as we will experience a multi-directional love that goes upward, outward and inward as we journey with God.

Thinking about the bigger picture, whenever we attempt to extend the influence of the Kingdom of Heaven on this earth, we will meet resistance on many levels. For example, politically where there is no acknowledgement of God, educationally where the Bible is removed from school, in healthcare where science is king, in society where Christianity is a minority, in family and friendships with those who are sceptical or against our message of good news, in spirituality where various other kingdoms of this world clash and war against us. This is why we must be convinced that what God calls us to do is indeed worthwhile, otherwise resistance could soon break us down. We do have a firm foundation and a solid rock on which to stand.

Jesus says three main things to his disciples: 1) to remember him in communion (Matt. 26:26-29), 2) to live as disciples ourselves, and 3) to make disciples of others through his great commission (Matt. 28:19-20). Of these, most churches or groups of disciples will regularly take communion together, attempt to live as disciples themselves but are often not focused on making disciples of others. Making disciples of others in commission is just as important as remembering Jesus in communion; and these are both the supernatural overflow of actually being a disciple. If we aren't making disciples of others then are we truly following Jesus, because that is exactly what he did? Willard believes that we must be intentional about making disciples.[29]

The following scriptures show us that a disciple must have a relationship with Father God and the desire to obey him... *"'Not everyone who says to me, "Lord, Lord," will enter the kingdom of heaven, but only the one who does the will of my Father who is in heaven'"* (Matt. 7:21), and... *"For whoever does the will of my Father in heaven is my brother and sister and mother"* (Matt. 12:50). Jesus has perfectly represented the Father to us and made access to him available... *"For through him we both have access to the Father by one Spirit"* (Eph. 2:18).

Whoever we spend a lot of time with, we will be influenced by and eventually become like. We must therefore spend time with Jesus. As we do so, we allow the Holy Spirit to aid us in being transformed to be like Jesus... *"And we all, who with unveiled faces contemplate the Lord's glory, are being*

---

[29] Willard, D. *The Divine Conspiracy*, P331.

transformed into his image with ever-increasing glory, which comes from the Lord, who is the Spirit" (2 Cor. 3:18). We must be spiritually alert to hear what he is speaking to us, so that we can follow his lead and move in his power... *"Since we live by the Spirit, let us keep in step with the Spirit"* (Gal. 5:25).

To make a disciple of someone else we have to teach them what we have learned. This will include demonstration and well as practical advice and learning scripture... *"And the things you have heard me say in the presence of many witnesses entrust to reliable people who will also be qualified to teach others"* (2 Tim. 2:2). Paul (a disciple) is teaching others (many witnesses) to teach others (reliable people) who are able to teach others (new disciples); covering four generations of disciples.

How did Jesus Make Disciples?

As we begin to focus on Matthew's Gospel, as was the case in my first book in this Kingdom Perspective Series, '*Territory of the Kingdom*', we can clearly see how Jesus went about making disciples. He did this through **demonstration** in Matthew chapter four, followed by **teaching** in chapters five to seven, which is again followed by some further **demonstration** in chapters eight and nine. Jesus did not only teach or only demonstrate his Kingdom – he did both! We can have Bible studies week after week that are full of great teaching, and whilst these are excellent of course, we must also expect to have to demonstrate his Kingdom. Paul says, that the kingdom of God is not a matter of talk but of power (1 Cor. 4:20). If we are going to be truly like Jesus, we should also expect to be demonstrating his spiritual power and authority.

It is also worth noting that in scripture this demonstration is usually to those who are not part of the Kingdom, which means those who don't know Jesus yet. We should enjoy God's presence and the miraculous when we do gather together as disciples, but also remember that God is not limited to working only there among us.

Are you convinced?

We must be convinced that we are supposed to make disciples. Being convinced means completely certain about something, and if we aren't then we won't do anything about it. I could say to you that it is right to be a good parent and you might nod and agree with me. But unless you are convinced of this you won't actually try and learn what that means, through reading books, taking advice, attending parenting seminars, and so applying yourself to good parenting practices. The same could be said of saving money. Great idea for sure, but unless you are convinced you won't start putting money into your savings account.

We won't become disciples let alone make disciples of others if we simply think it's a good idea. We do have to be convinced it is a great idea and God's commission for all disciples of Jesus, otherwise, we will not commit our lives to this. It will be easier to have the attitude that says as long as this doesn't overly or adversely affect my lifestyle or my comforts – then yes, it's a great concept – but still not feel you have to personally do anything about it. But if you are convinced that you are a disciple that is to make disciples, then you will do something about it. Hull and Sobels concur... "*if we truly believed in disciple making, we would be making disciples, not excuses*".[30]

In the OT the word 'disciple' is mentioned in Isaiah... "*Bind up this testimony of warning and seal up God's instruction among my disciples*" (Isa. 8:16). The Hebrew word is *lamad* from the root word *limmud*, meaning accustomed or taught. The word is found twice more in Isaiah (50:4; 54:13) and twice in Jeremiah (2:24; 13:23). However, in the NT, the word 'disciple' is mentioned much more often: in the Gospels – Matthew seventy-six times, Mark fifty-eight times, Luke forty-seven times and John seventy-two times – and also in the book of Acts twenty-six times. The Greek word used is *mathetai* from the root word *mathetes*, meaning a follower of Christ who learns the doctrines of scripture **and the lifestyle they require**. This word is found elsewhere in the NT and it is usually translated as 'learner' or 'to learn'.

Jesus was himself a disciple

Before any disciples were selected or called by Jesus, he was first a disciple himself... "*Jesus gave them this answer: "Very truly I tell you, the Son can do nothing by himself; he can do only what he sees his Father doing, because whatever the Father does the Son also does*" (John 5:19), and... "*By myself I can do nothing; I judge only as I hear, and my judgment is just, for I seek not to please myself but him who sent me*" (John 5:30).

Jesus saw the Father, I would suggest through impressions, pictures and visions (moving spiritual scenes). Jesus would

---

[30] Hull, B., Sobels, B. *The Discipleship Gospel*, P98.

learn from him and do the same. Jesus also heard the Father, and I would suggest at times his audible voice, as well as his still small whisper (because he was listening), to be able to continue in obedience to the Father's will. Simply put, Jesus did what the Father asked him to do. Now if we are disciples learning to become more like Jesus we should also be learning to hear God's voice, to see what he does and obey what he asks of us. We will look into this in more detail in chapter nine of this second section.

The Call to discipleship

"*As Jesus was walking beside the Sea of Galilee, he saw two brothers, Simon called Peter and his brother Andrew. They were casting a net into the lake, for they were fishermen.* [19] '*Come,* **follow me**,' *Jesus said, 'and I will send you out to fish for people.'* [20] *At once they left their nets and followed him.* [21] *Going on from there, he saw two other brothers, James son of Zebedee and his brother John. They were in a boat with their father Zebedee, preparing their nets. Jesus called them,* [22] *and immediately they left the boat and their father and followed him*" (Matt. 4:18-22).

When Jesus calls his first disciples the actual word 'disciple' is not used but this is what he is doing. Some Bible translations have a title for this section of scripture called, "Calling his first Disciples". The parallel story is found in Mark chapter one.

The first thing we notice is that their location is by the Sea of Galilee, which is a significant place for Israel and which had been in great darkness. Yet it becomes the first place where the discipleship making, Jesus style, would start. It is often called 'the Sea' but it is only thirteen miles (21km) long by eight miles

(13km) wide, and so is also referred to in scripture as 'the Lake'. In the physical or natural this was an incredibly fertile region, and so the darkness experienced there related to its spiritual climate.

Jesus was walking beside the sea or lake, presumably on dry ground, when he sees Simon who would later be called Peter and his brother Andrew. They were casting a net which means that they were working – perhaps standing in shallow water or sitting in a boat. Fishing has not changed much over the centuries and is still seen today by many, as a hard manual, low skilled and smelly job! Jesus looks past the lowly, poorly educated brothers and instead sees their hearts. What kind of jobs have you had? Your actual work, no matter how lowly it might be considered (or even lack of work), has nothing to do with your ability to be called as a disciple of Jesus. This is not an excuse that you can use (Matt. 4:18).

Jesus said, "*Come, follow me*", it could not get much simpler, could it? Follow did not mean just track where I go, but become like me, **walk as I walk**, be my disciple... "*and I will send you out to fish for people*". Simon and Andrew knew their trade and Jesus used the thing they knew how to do best, to give them the spark of motivation that they perhaps needed – fishing for a greater cause. At once, *eutheos*, they obeyed and left. Leaving everything and everyone behind.

I once worked with both my son Carl and my daughter Sasha in company offices in the town of Reading, Berkshire. They were both working in the accounts department and I was working in IT. Now imagine if Jesus walked in to their office and said "come follow me", and... "I will send you out to account for people". Then they simply obeyed, immediately got up, and walked out of the office never to return! Both the ancient and the modern-day equivalent example are rather bizarre situations don't you think? Yet, what Jesus does is to take something that we are most familiar with and skilled at, and uses that thing for a much greater and higher purpose. Interestingly, Jesus calls to the disciples which is the opposite of a Jewish Rabbi whose disciples had to approach and attach themselves to the Rabbi (Matt. 4:19).

Jesus' simple instruction to follow him or be his disciple is followed by being sent out of our normal locale. We cannot stay inside the four walls of our church; Jesus sends us out to people...we are to be disciples on mission (Matt. 4:20).

James and John, the sons of Zebedee, were in a boat preparing or mending their nets as commercial fishermen just like Simon and Andrew. Andrew himself is not mentioned much more in scripture but he is the one who asked about the fish and loaves to feed the five thousand... "*another of his disciples, Andrew, Simon Peter's brother, spoke up, 'Here is a boy with five small barley loaves and two small fish, but how far will they go among so many?'*" (John 6:8-9). Jesus calls James and John too and we might assume that he used the same simple instruction, but the text does not tell us his actual words (Matt. 4:21). Again, they also just leave the family business, the rest of their family and friends. They do this immediately – the same word *eutheos* is used; they obeyed and left (Matt. 4:22). Simon and this second pair of brothers, James and John, go on to become the closest disciples of Jesus. It is they alone who got to witness Jesus miraculously raising Jairus' daughter from the dead, Jesus' most incredible and spectacular transfiguration on the mountain, and his anguish in the garden of Gethsemane.

Why were these four rough and ready blokes so convinced? Jesus asked them to give up everything – their livelihood and family – to follow Him. It was an extreme cost and a massive risk. Why would they do it? Was it the way he looked or the tone of his voice when he asked? Was he a great salesman? I think we may need a revelation like these four blokes must have had – and I believe it is so profoundly simple...**Jesus is God**! We also recognise that these and any tradesmen would have been rejected by Rabbis at the end of their education as not being good enough, only the 'cream of the crop' being allowed to continue to a higher learning under them. Both sets of brothers were learning their trade from their fathers who would have also previously been rejected in this way. Now a different type of Rabbi comes to them and says "*come follow me*", presenting them with an opportunity that could not be turned down, as they finally receive value and worth in their culture.

God had come to planet earth and stood in front of them – no nice introduction: "Hi my name's Jesus and I'm a carpenter from Nazareth" – no handshake or high five! Jesus stood there asking them to give up everything they thought was good because he simply wanted devoted disciples, not half-hearted followers, but those who would be willing to sacrifice anything for him.

If Jesus was here physically right now and asking the same of you, how do you think you would respond? Perhaps you too would leave everything and follow him and go out full-time into the mission field. Well, he is here. Through the power of the Holy Spirit, Jesus is not only here in our midst but he lives inside you (Col. 1:27). If Jesus is the same yesterday, today and forever (Heb. 13:8) then do you think he would change his request? No, it is still the same request today. But perhaps we are not hearing him say it. The noise of life, the turmoil within, the spiritual darkness, the apathy, the desire for self-first shouts louder than Jesus is speaking. Turn inwards and listen. Stop the noise and listen. Give him your innermost being and let him create in you a pure heart (Psalm 51:10) and a healthy heart, then listen and obey his requests.

Of course, our individual calling may vary – pastor, teacher, prophet, evangelist, apostle. Discipleship is for all, not only for the evangelist or full-time overseas missionary. We must all see ourselves as apprentices, called in word and power, to go into our current spheres of influence. Even if we are never called to quit our jobs or change our physical locale to another part of this world, we are all called to make a difference wherever Jesus has placed us.

Willard believes that it is possible to be a professing Christian without being a disciple,[31] and yet, aren't we supposed to be his ambassadors? Those accredited as diplomatic agents of the highest rank by heaven, as a permanent representative of it, into this world. People living in a foreign land (we are in this

---

[31] Willard, D. *The Divine Conspiracy*, P319.

world but not of it), who promote heavens activities here... *"We are therefore Christ's ambassadors, as though God were making his appeal through us"* (2 Cor. 5:20). It is worth noting, that Ambassador happens to be a title that is retained for life.

In Conclusion

We have seen what a disciple or citizen of the Kingdom of Heaven is. We must be convinced that we are one, so that we will indeed action what we are meant to do, even during times of resistance. Our response is to obey the call to follow him, to be a disciple and make more disciples. Jesus was himself a disciple who set us this example and standard. It seems that our job, education and social background are not relevant when it comes to being called. A disciple gets to know Jesus and then goes out on mission to learn and to serve him. What Jesus found in these ordinary working-class people was those who would sacrificially give all of themselves. They were **willing** and they made themselves **available** to Jesus.

We are all called by him to be disciples, his ambassadors or representatives of heaven, who must learn patience, something that fishermen seem to have in plenty – they know how to wait. They fished with nets, not by using a line which only catches one fish at a time. In a similar way, Jesus sends us out into the mission field to the multitudes. Jesus does not make this easy, but he was and is so convincing that they, and we, almost have no choice but to respond with our immediate obedience. We should be just like Isaiah, who six-hundred years before Jesus, saw Jesus in a vision and responded... *"Here am I. Send me!"* (Isa. 6:8).

CHAPTER TWO

Citizens Are Enthusiastic Not Hesitant

Jesus gathered around him those that he had called, and he began to demonstrate and to teach them the laws of the Kingdom that they had now entered. We find these topsy turvy and radical laws of love, that so challenged the thinking and understanding of the Pharisees, in the Sermon on the Mount (Matt. 5-7). Interestingly, in the three chapters of the Sermon, the word 'disciple' is only mentioned once in the very first verse when his disciples came to him (Matt. 5:1).

The action-packed chapters eight and nine of Matthew take place in Galilee. When the first healings are performed, the people living there hear of them and they become hopeful and go to Jesus, and Jesus heals them all. This underlines Jesus' authority as the King of his Kingdom, which he taught about and is now fully demonstrating. Chapter seven ended after his extended teaching... *"the crowds were amazed at his teaching, because he taught as one who had authority"* (Matt. 7:29). Jesus then demonstrates this authority as an example for his disciples back then to see, and for us to continue today.

In chapter eight we see Jesus come down from the mountain and again go into demonstration mode, but this time with increased intensity. First, he heals a man with leprosy, then heals the paralysed servant of the faith-filled Roman centurion from a distance, he heals Peter's mother-in-law of a fever, then from many he cast out demons, he healed all the sick fulfilling Isaiah's prophecy about himself – astonishing! (Matt. 8:1-17).

If we go back and include chapter four, in which Jesus had called his first disciples and then immediately healed every disease and sickness, including those who were suffering from demon possession, we see what resembles an amazing type of sandwich. Sandwich! You may now be laughing or at least wondering what on earth I might mean, but this is what we see:

Demonstration
Teaching
Demonstration

It is almost hidden within these two outstanding chapters eight and nine, that we see cycles of amazing healings and miracles interwoven with the true cost or challenge of being a disciple of Jesus. There are twelve such amazing stories within which the discipleship challenges can be lost if we are not paying attention. Perhaps Matthew included twelve, one for each of the tribes of Israel or the first disciples. Matthew was writing his account to Jewish Christians to give them instruction on how to live in this new Kingdom, that Jesus had ushered in, as they began to face persecution. Therefore, much of the language used is meaningful and very relevant to those original recipients. Here is a list of these twelve incredible ministry moments, in which Jesus seems to increase the wonders of his ministry and what he could do, as he demonstrates the Kingdom to his disciples:

Chapter eight... 1) healing what was then an incurable disease of leprosy through touch, 2) healing from a distance the Roman centurion's servant, 3) healing Peter's mother-in-law who is much closer and well known to this group of disciples – so it's not just random strangers any longer, 4) casting out demons from many people and healing all the sick who came to him, 5) first nature miracle – calming a storm, and 6) casting a legion of demons from the Gadarene demonic, into a herd of pigs who then all drown.

Chapter nine... 7) healing a Paralytic, 8) Raising the Synagogue Ruler's daughter from the dead, 9) healing woman with an unstoppable haemorrhage, 10) healing two blind men, 11) exorcising a dumb demoniac, and 12) in towns, villages and synagogues – preaching the Kingdom and healing every single disease and sickness.

It is no wonder therefore that it is easy to miss the discipleship challenges and lessons that Jesus teaches, hidden among the miracles, as we can simply be carried away with the miraculous ministry of Jesus. These gems are there to be found and it is my hope that by highlighting them, we will learn more about being and making disciples. We will now pick up the text in verse eighteen of chapter eight, where Jesus is being quite abrupt in bringing an emphasis to the cost of authentic discipleship.

It's costly to follow Jesus

"*When Jesus saw the crowd around him, he gave orders to cross to the other side of the lake. [19] Then a teacher of the law came to him and said, 'Teacher, I will follow you wherever you go.' [20] Jesus replied, 'Foxes have dens and birds have nests, but the*

Son of Man has nowhere to lay his head.' [21] *Another disciple said to him, 'Lord, first let me go and bury my father.'* [22] *But Jesus told him, '***Follow me, and let the dead bury their own dead.***'"* (Matt. 8:18-22).

In the midst of this amazing demonstration of ministry, the like of which had never been seen before, Jesus does not stand around and wait for applause or the approval of man, as some of the great modern-day actors or sports stars do. Neither does he take up an offering so that he can gain financially, like many of the prosperity type ministries that we unfortunately see. Instead, he simply looks to move on, to cross over the lake (which would have been the Sea of Galilee), to go where his Father asks him to go. I wonder where is Papa asking you to go and if are you obeying him?

Jesus here gave orders. Does that surprise you, that Jesus would give orders? Well, it shouldn't do, because every King gives orders to his subjects, to his citizens. I'm sure that he would have used the right tone and continued to love, but nonetheless, he still gave them. Jesus knew what the next part of his ministry and discipleship journey would be, both on the lake (calming a storm) and the other side of it (casting out a legion of demons), so he now wants to provide them with a preparatory object lesson (Matt. 8:18).

Superficial Enthusiasm

Before Jesus gets the chance to board, a teacher of the law, a rabbi, comes to Jesus. This rabbi is super enthusiastic and who wouldn't be...put yourself into the story for a moment and imagine being there and seeing all these incredible healings and deliverances from demons, and many people being set free – the amazement, the joy, the awe, the wonder! Perhaps in a similar but smaller way, I remember the look of complete amazement on the face of a young woman in her mid-twenties in Estonia, when we prayed in church for her damaged knees. She tested them by squatting down and up a few times to realise that they didn't hurt anymore – she was healed! Then after the church service had finished and we were heading to our cars, we heard that her back was also causing her a lot of pain. We prayed. The next day she went to the gym and was able to train without any pain in her back.

We can easily get carried away with miracles but they are not the true heart of the Kingdom. Please don't get me wrong, we should absolutely expect, see and demonstrate the spectacular signs of the Kingdom. Miracles today are signposts to Jesus after all. What I mean, is that if we only seek these things for an in-house (church) entertainment factor, or seek some kind of glory for ourselves in them, then we are not true disciples... *"Not everyone who says to me, 'Lord, Lord,' will enter the kingdom of heaven, but only the one who does the will of my Father who is in heaven. Many will say to me on that day, 'Lord, Lord, did we not prophesy in your name and in your name drive out demons and in your name perform many miracles?' Then I will tell them plainly, 'I never knew you. Away from me, you evildoers!"* (Matt. 7:21-23). Rather we should be prepared to give up even our creature comforts if that is what the King requires of us.

So, this enthusiastic rabbi declares boldly *"Teacher, I will follow you wherever you go"*. A rabbi was highly regarded in Jewish culture and still is today. He taught the Law of Moses and was someone who knew the OT rule book. He calls Jesus 'teacher' and so it is likely he had overheard in the crowds all that Jesus had just taught earlier on the mountainside. But now he sees with his own eyes a new Kingdom being demonstrated and the authority of Jesus as a work in practice. So suddenly the rabbi, the teacher of the old law, wants to become the student of this amazing new law. He recognised a new thing and perhaps even recognised this as the new and better way, a new covenant from and with God.

When we first meet Jesus and realise who he actually is i.e. God, and we first fall in love with him, we may have felt like this enthusiastic rabbi. Perhaps we too declared that we would follow him everywhere. Do you remember that, and did it work out that way in the reality of your life? Possibly not. When you first fell in love or got married, perhaps you didn't realise the cost and commitment of what you had just signed up for. Later that reality kicks in, that it's a lifetime of hard work and self-sacrifice (Matt. 8:19).

This is what Jesus is saying in his response to this potential new disciple. The enthusiastic rabbi gets an immediate reality check of the cost, in other words...salvation is free but discipleship will cost you your life! This legal expert makes his promise based on his own quick-thinking initiative. Jesus' response is also quick and to the point. Jesus sees the heart of people and could see what was really within this rabbi. He replies saying that "*Foxes have dens and birds have nests, but the Son of Man has nowhere to lay his head*". Jesus points to the fact that he is giving up all comfort to go on a three-year journey of itinerant mission and ministry to those that are outcasts, misfits, the oppressed, the rejected, the poor and the lowly. He was willing not to even have a place to sleep or a place to call home, which even the animals have. Ultimately, he will lay down his life for the cause of his Kingdom. Now before you judge this rabbi, please let me put you in his shoes. Give me the keys to your house and your car (or cars), leave everything that you know and people you love, quit your job, no need for that credit card so you might as well leave me the PIN code. Now just start walking wherever the Holy Spirit leads you. Are you ready? It's not that easy to be a disciple of Jesus. There is a huge cost to your life and your all. The same degree of surrender is required even if you are not called into full-time service.

We can probably conclude that the rabbi only had a superficial enthusiasm, which Jesus saw and brought a challenge to. The rabbi had not counted the true cost of discipleship. Again, before judging, how is your discipleship doing? What is it costing you? Is there any sacrifice? Are you giving everything or even anything up for the cause of the Kingdom?

Interestingly, Jesus uses the title 'Son of Man' of himself. The rabbi would have known of this title from the prophet Daniel, when the Ancient of Days (God the Father), gives his Kingdom to his Son. This is the first time that this title appears in Matthew, and by using it, Jesus declares himself to be God because the Son is the exact representation of the Father. Jesus taught with authority, demonstrated his authority and then declares his authority. He is our King! Yet this King who is the Saviour, the Messiah, the anointed one, the healer – is also a homeless itinerant missionary living by faith and relying upon

God to provide any creature comforts in this life, through the hospitality of others (Matt. 8:20).

Don't Hesitate

Next, another disciple said to him... "*Lord, first let me go and bury my father*". We do not know whose disciple this was, but he could have been following the super-enthusiastic rabbi perhaps. This potential disciple of Jesus also wants to follow Jesus, and he does appear in this story, to have a better grasp of the cost this might entail. However, when he realises the high price, he hesitates. He is unsure, not convinced, and wants to delay walking (or sailing) on with Jesus. He decides to make a really valid excuse. I'm sure that we would be happy with its validity. He has to go to the funeral of one of his closet relatives. But in doing this his natural father's funeral is therefore taking the priority over following Jesus. Jesus sees through the 'smoke and mirrors' and looks at the heart. He sees a person that is not fully in or wholehearted. How about you? Jesus demands immediate and total loyalty to himself and his Kingdom, and yet we can remain anxious in fully committing ourselves to Jesus (Matt. 8:21).

Jesus told him... "*Follow me, and let the dead bury their own dead*". Wow, that seems really harsh, doesn't it? Essentially, I believe that Jesus is saying to let those who are not completely sold out to the Kingdom take care of the burial. Those who are spiritually dead, and dead to the Kingdom, can bury those that have died physically. This does not mean that someone completely committed to the Kingdom cannot either take or go to a funeral service. Jesus must be our first priority, even over very important matters. I know many missionaries who are based overseas and in the Covid-19 pandemic were not able to travel home to say goodbye to loved ones that have died. Such a tough situation. However, this concept is not new to us: we are to love God above everything else as seen in the first and greatest commandment (Matt. 22:37 which quotes Deut. 6:5), and is therefore found in both the OT and the NT (Matt. 8:22).

In Conclusion

Enthusiastic but superficial and only surface level discipleship is not enough. It has to be such a deep life-transforming thing that we learn self-sacrifice and complete devotion. Emotional enthusiasm, in and of itself, is not sufficient and does not properly consider the demands of being a disciple who walks with Jesus.

Hesitant discipleship is also not enough. Having a realistic understanding of the cost and the sacrifice that Jesus calls us to can make us hesitate and sit on the fence. We can use very good reasons not to move forward in our walk with Father, Son and Holy Spirit. The demands of the King and his Kingdom should even revise our notion of whose family we belong to.

These stories show us that ignorance of the cost, or being non-committal when knowing the cost, leads to the same result. Both of these types of disciple, the superficially enthusiastic and the hesitant, are disqualified. If you want to gain an authentic PhD it will likely cost you four years of full-time hard and dedicated study. It is exactly the same with authentic discipleship. If you enthusiastically and without hesitation commit to following what Jesus commands, then you are his true and authentic disciple. If you know and are willing to count the cost, by gladly choosing this difficult and narrow path that your King leads you down, you will walk in the most incredible Kingdom of love and power.

CHAPTER THREE

Citizens Are Obedient and Merciful

After Jesus says that both enthusiasm alone and hesitancy are not enough to make a disciple (Matt. 8:18-22), we next see him 'up the ante' somewhat, by speaking to nature itself – and even that obeys him. Jesus and his crew have boarded the boat to sail across the lake during which a violent storm blows in and it is a bad one, with waves crashing over the boat. The Greek word that Matthew uses, *seismos*, means upheaval – an upheaval of the waters. The lake or Sea of Galilee that they were crossing has high hills around it, and strong winds would suddenly blow through like a giant funnel and cause a storm. Jesus gets up and rebukes; the word is *epetimesen*, which means to censure or to forbid. The wind and the waves disappear and it is immediately calm again (Matt. 8:23-27). Is there a circumstance in which you do not have peace? Is there turmoil in your life? Jesus is able to bring a certain and complete inward calm, regardless of what the circumstances surrounding and engulfing happen to be. In every storm that shakes us, we can find peace. The world might be in a Covid-19 storm, but we can live in the presence and peace of Jesus and demonstrate that calmness to those who don't know him and may be panicking. In this particular case, Jesus decides to totally remove the storm.

Next, Jesus easily heals two super-demonised men (Matt. 8:28-34) which demonstrates his authority over the supernatural realm. Then he forgives sin which is only something that God can do, as he also heals a paralysed man (Matt. 9:1-8).

The Calling of Matthew

"As Jesus went on from there, he saw a man named Matthew sitting at the tax collector's booth. 'Follow me,' he told him, and Matthew got up and followed him. [10] While Jesus was having dinner at Matthew's house, many tax collectors and sinners came and ate with him and his disciples. [11] When the Pharisees saw this, they asked his disciples, 'Why does your teacher eat with tax collectors and sinners?' [12] On hearing this, Jesus said, 'It is not the healthy who need a doctor, but those who are ill. [13] But go and learn what this means: "I desire mercy, not sacrifice." For I have not come to call the righteous, but sinners.'" (Matt. 9:9-13).

Jesus crosses the lake or Sea of Galilee in chapter eight to heal the two demoniacs, after which he returns to his home town of Nazareth (Matt. 9:1). This is where he sets out from in our story above. The leaders there questioned what Jesus did and accused him of blasphemy. It was a place that later amazed Jesus for its complete lack of faith (Matt. 13:54-58).

Taxes back then, in first-century Israel, would have been collected at various locations like ports, important crossroads, places of commerce, and by city gates. Perhaps Jesus sees Matthew for the first time sitting in his tax collecting booth as he either left Nazareth or joined the nearest important cross-road. Tax collectors could walk up to a man and tax him for what he was carrying, or the goods he was transporting. They had a reputation of being corrupt, crooked and thieves who unfairly extorted money from ordinary people. No Jew would want this job because they collected taxes on behalf of a hated foreign ruler and power over their nation – Rome. These tax collectors were hated and despised because they were usually fellow Jews who were traitors now working for Rome. Perhaps the most famous tax collector is Zacchaeus (Luke 19:1-10), but did you realise that the tax-collecting Matthew here is actually the famous writer of the first gospel? He is describing his own call to follow Jesus.

At the call of his first disciples back in chapter four, Jesus calls simple, hardworking fishermen. Now Jesus wants to recruit a known sinner! Why would that be? Perhaps no one else would reach out to these outcasts within Jewish society itself. Jesus always reached out to the orphan, the widow and these outcast groups – he simply wouldn't ignore them. He looked beyond their lifestyle, job or sinful behaviour and saw potential. He wanted a people that were united and cared for, which sounds a bit like Moses in his utopian vision for Israel found in the Book of Deuteronomy before Israel entered the Promised Land.

Being Obedient

Jesus tells Matthew, "*follow me*". Short and sweet but clearly effective, as we see that Matthew does just that. This gospel recorder does not give any hesitation, nor is he superficially enthusiastic, but rather gives immediate obedience (Matt. 9:9).

It would seem that by dinnertime Jesus has been invited to Matthew's house for something to eat. This would have been the hospitable thing to do. As a tax collector Matthew would likely have been wealthy and have a nice place to live in and great tasting food on offer. He had friends in the same line of work, who would have formed their own group of the unpopular, who most likely would have stuck together as reasonably well-to-do friends. There were also 'sinners' that had come to dine with them; whilst this could refer to the tax collectors, there may have been those from other walks of life that had also been labelled as sinners.

Today we might think such a category would include drug dealers, those extorting money from the poor and vulnerable, drunkards, prostitutes or even politicians. How many of us have friends, and I mean friendly enough to invite over for a meal, who are labelled as sinners? We probably don't mix with them very much and mainly have our friendships with those inside the church. We can become so used to being around only church friends that we clam up in our faith when we get our hair cut or go to the supermarket and have the opportunity to talk with sinners. Remember though, that Paul in his letter to the believers in Rome tells us that all have sinned, and that includes us (Rom. 3:23). As disciples, we need to get over ourselves a little bit and see that we need to help rescue outcasts. Jesus and his disciples were all happy to sit with this group, spend time with them and share their food, which was an important value in Jewish culture.

Have we grown up in the church where there were many rules, like not being allowed to go to a party or the cinema, just in case there are 'bad' people there who might influence us into ungodly behaviour? My response to that is twofold: 1) that you can go where your godly conscious allows you to go but avoid places of personal temptation, and don't go alone so that you have someone to be accountable to, and 2) when you do go, represent Jesus and the Kingdom of Heaven with a particular desire to be an intentional light in a dark place (Matt. 9:10).

Being Merciful

This meal at Matthew's house did not go unnoticed by the religious leaders. It wasn't done in secret, and for Jesus this was probably intentional. He breaks a social taboo which is something seen as repulsive by those who defined the Jewish culture and its laws. The Pharisees are so offended that they don't ask Jesus directly – what on earth is going on? No, they ask his disciples instead (Matt. 9:11).

The disciples then seem to pass on the message and Jesus answers them. He says that it is precisely the spiritually unhealthy people, the outcasts if you like, or those not knowing Jesus, who are the ones that the doctor needs to go to. Doctors help sick people. Jesus here is going to those who need some intensive care. As we mature into healthy disciples we should not need as much help from others. We of course will always be dependent upon the Holy Spirit for our close relationship and dialogue with God. However, we all still need those ahead of us in our journey to mentor us, but intrinsically, we need to be going to the sick and taking the light of Doctor Jesus to those who are not spiritually healthy, including those we might prefer not to mix with. We are a sent people. We are a disciple-making people too (Matt. 9:12).

Jesus tells his disciples to learn the true meaning of the words "*I desire mercy, not sacrifice*". This comes from Hosea chapter six. **Justice** gives people what they do in fact deserve. In a court of law, if you are found guilty, you will be sentenced so that justice is served. **Mercy,** however, shows compassion and forgiveness towards someone over whom we have the power to judge, punish or harm. For Jesus, **sacrifice** is also very important. Our time, energy, money and commitment, he does want, but he is saying that he would rather you go and show mercy to others than continue to bring your sacrifices to him. You see we can write people off as outcasts and still continue with our sacrifices, both day in and day out. Jesus wants us to extend his love to others ahead of giving him our sacrifices. That is not instead of, but ahead of. We still make sacrifices but often we have the priority the wrong way round. As disciples of Jesus, we are first a 'sent' people, sent even to those that society classes as outcasts or unlovable, to tell them about our wonderful Lord and Saviour, and to show them compassion. Being a disciple means learning to show mercy – to live mercifully.

Jesus did not come to earth to call 'the righteous' to himself. He had his harshest words for the Pharisees and religious leaders who were leading people into religious bondage. They saw themselves as being the righteous ones because they knew and interpreted the OT law. Jesus, in contrast, would not turn anyone away who wished to truly count the cost and follow him – but he goes to those who are willing to realise that they need help, like a doctor perhaps, a saviour from their sin, or someone who could put them in right standing with Papa – with Father God. Only Jesus can do this. He also brings the outcast home and gives them new life and a new identity in him. The righteous ones incorrectly thought that observing the law would save them (Matt. 9:13).

In Conclusion

Citizens obey their King. The Bible does show us that if we do obey, not just from a place of having to, but by really wanting to, then we will be blessed – blessed in many ways but especially in a living and vibrant relationship with our beautiful King, the most amazing heavenly Father, and the Holy Spirit who walks alongside us as we journey this life. Not all our troubles will be removed but we will stay close in our walk with God. We have learnt that we need to be immediately obedient as Matthew testified of his own calling. I have heard it said that even delayed obedience is disobedience. Disciples are obedient and we obey our King.

So, what is it that our King asks of us? We have seen that we are sent to go where sinners are and meet them as we find them and to make friends with them. As we do so, we don't judge either their condition or their situation. Instead, we take the one person to them, that can make them healthy. We bring the light of Jesus into their dark world to rescue them and to make disciples of them. Doing these things will require us to show mercy. We do have the power to help people but we can easily hinder them, especially if we ignore them or refuse to associate with them. When we do this as our first priority, then when we take our sacrifices to Jesus, he will gladly accept them.

Jesus too learnt obedience through the many trials that he went through. At one point he even asked the Father if there could be another way (Luke 22:42). Jesus on earth, stayed obedient to his Father and remained true to his heavenly Kingdom and calling. He was untainted by any other dark kingdom of this world. In doing so, Jesus ushered in a heavenly Kingdom on earth for all humanity to reach out and grab hold of. Without Jesus' obedience, all for us would be lost. And so, our treasure should be in this heavenly Kingdom. We get the most amazing opportunity to participate in it, and also to demonstrate its power on this earth. This will require our obedience and it occurs when we are merciful. Putting this Kingdom on display will allow others, even the outcasts, to taste and see that the Lord is good (Psalm 34:8).

CHAPTER FOUR

Citizens Fast

Having seen that citizens of the Kingdom are convinced, enthusiastic, not hesitant, but obedient and merciful, we next see that citizens are to fast. We will not be doing an in-depth study on fasting but looking primarily at the heart motivation behind it.

"Then John's disciples came and asked him, 'How is it that we and the Pharisees fast often, but your disciples do not fast?' [15] *Jesus answered, 'How can the guests of the bridegroom mourn while he is with them? The time will come when the bridegroom will be taken from them; then they will fast.* [16] *'No one sews a patch of unshrunk cloth on an old garment, for the patch will pull away from the garment, making the tear worse.* [17] *Neither do people pour new wine into old wineskins. If they do, the skins will burst; the wine will run out, and the wineskins will be ruined. No, they pour new wine into new wineskins, and both are preserved.'"* (Matt. 9:14-17).

The Question

It would seem that Jesus is still enjoying his dinner with the outcasts when he is approached by a group of John the Baptists' disciples who have a burning question to ask. They want to understand why it is that the religious leaders regularly fast to fulfil the requirements of the law, that one of the annual festivals requires all Jews to fast, that they too as disciples of

103

John also fasted, and yet this is not the case for the disciples following Jesus. Strange?

John's disciples were much more closely aligned with, and accepting of Jesus, and his ministry than the Pharisees were. They believed in a baptism of repentance and lived as those under the OT law. They had essentially become those who sat in between these two positions, but they were crucially not against Jesus and felt that they could approach him and ask their question directly.

Up to this point in Matthew, we have only seen Jesus' personal forty-day water only fast (Matt. 4:1-2), and then his reference to fasting, and that he expects it, in the Sermon on the Mount (Matt. 6:16-18). Yet it appears that fasting is not being particularly pushed by Jesus, nor seemingly volunteered by his disciples, otherwise John's disciples would not have had that specific question.

Only one fast was commanded in the law of Moses. On the Day of Atonement, the whole nation was to deny themselves by abstaining from food and water (Lev. 16:29). In the time period that Jesus walked this earth, the Pharisees would additionally attempt to live out this law by fasting two days per week (Luke 18:12). Fasting on Mondays and Thursdays was a tradition they practised. This fasting was a source of pride among the Pharisees who would even boast about it. This may have been exactly the type of fasting that John's disciples had also adopted. What was their motive for asking this question? For the Pharisees, it was always from the wrong heart and for some kind of entrapment. For John's disciples, it was more likely asked in genuine ignorance and for also furthering their understanding.

Those who practised fasting out of a mechanical religion were oblivious to the fact that they were living in the age of the Messiah, a time that Israel had expected to be a joyous marriage-feast type of time-period in history. It's a little ironic that they ask this question when Jesus is doing just that: feasting.

The principal reason and true purpose for fasting is spiritual. **Fasting is all about seeking God with the right heart motive as we live out his heart desires**. Trust good old Isaiah to lead the way on this, for Israel in the OT, for the religious in Jesus' era, and very much so for us still today... "*Shout it aloud, do not hold back. Raise your voice like a trumpet. Declare to my people their rebellion and to the descendants of Jacob their sins.² For day after day they seek me out; they seem eager to know my ways, as if they were a nation that does what is right and has not forsaken the commands of its God. They ask me for just decisions and seem eager for God to come near them. ³ "Why have we fasted," they say, "and you have not seen it? Why have we humbled ourselves, and you have not noticed?" Yet on the day of your fasting, you do as you please and exploit all your workers.⁴ Your fasting ends in quarrelling and strife, and in striking each other with wicked fists. You cannot fast as you do today and expect your voice to be heard on high.⁵ Is this the kind of fast I have chosen, only a day for people to humble themselves? Is it only for bowing one's head like a reed and for lying in sackcloth and ashes? Is that what you call a fast, a day acceptable to the Lord? ⁶ Is not this the kind of fasting I have chosen: to loose the* *chains of injustice and untie the cords of the yoke, to set the oppressed free and break every yoke?[7] Is it not to share your food with the hungry and to provide the poor wanderer with shelter – when you see the naked, to clothe them, and not to turn away from your own flesh and blood?[8]* Then your light will break forth like the dawn, and your healing will quickly appear; then your righteousness will go before you, and the glory of the Lord will be your rear guard.[9] **Then you will call, and the Lord will answer; you will cry for help, and he will say: here am I**" (Isa. 58:1-9).

Types of Fasts

There are several different types of fast that we find in the Bible. There is a 'Supernatural Fast', where people go without food and water for long periods of time, like Moses when he received the ten commandments (Exod. 34:28). There is an 'Absolute Fast', where people go without food and water for one to three days, like when Esther asked the Jews in Susa to fast for her (Esth. 4:16), or Saul after his conversion (Acts 9:9). There is a 'Normal Fast', where people abstain from food, solids (or liquidised form), but not from water, like Jesus during his forty days of temptation in the wilderness (Luke 4:2). There is a 'Partial Fast', where the emphasis is upon restriction of food and liquids for a longer period for example ten days, rather than a complete abstention, as Daniel and his friends did (Dan. 1:12).

The one thing in common is that virtually every fast comes to an end and is broken. Every morning we are probably fortunate enough to have 'Break-Fast', after a night's sleep. There are times though when people are involuntary forced into fasts, in dire poverty or prisoner of war camps. There are also those who voluntarily fast in a hunger strike, for a cause they believe in so much that they are willing to die for it. Fasting is a serious business indeed and should therefore not be undertaken either religiously or lightly.

I know people who have done a forty-day water only fast. I'm not sure that I would attempt one, unless I knew with certainty God was asking me to. I have done normal fluid only fasts over a number of days on several occasions, and usually do a partial fruit and veg. only fast for twenty-one days before any overseas mission trip. I sometimes do these at the start of a new year church wide fast. Once, I felt that God had asked me to preach a Good Friday message by hammering large nails into a life size cross, strapping it up and getting on it! There was a small block already fixed on which I stood as I held onto the nails with my hands. From the cross I shouted out the seven statements that are attributed to Jesus in scripture, which I had memorised. It was a powerful moment that brought to life the reality of the cross. It is not something I ever expect to repeat. God had spoken to me nine or ten months before Easter and I wrestled with this whole idea during that time. I did not feel that I could do it, but was determined to keep listening and to be obedient. I did a partial fluid only fast for twenty days leading up to that Good Friday. Without the fasting I really don't think I would have been able to do what God had asked me to.

The Answers

Going back to Jesus' response to John's disciples, we see that his answer was threefold and he uses three different images to explain why his disciples don't fast like the disciples of John and the Pharisees. At the same time, Jesus reveals something of the radically new nature of his Kingdom.

In Jesus' first answer, he declares that he is the bridegroom and therefore his disciples are the guests of the bridegroom. It would not be fitting for the guests of the bridegroom to fast or mourn while the bridegroom is present with them. Can you imagine today being at a wedding banquet that you have been invited to, but people attending are refusing to eat the wonderfully delicious food provided? Now that would be strange! Yet in this response, Jesus is also making a startling claim of deity, to being God, that we can easily skip over. The OT uses this same type of language to describe God's relationship with the nation of Israel... "*I will betroth you to Me forever; Yes, I will betroth you to Me in righteousness and justice, in loving-kindness and mercy; I will betroth you to Me in faithfulness, And you shall know the LORD*" (Hos. 2:19-20). Jesus is using this same language to declare that he is in fact the bridegroom who will call to himself a bride, those in Israel and the Church, made up of believing Jews and Gentiles. This long-expected promise of the prophet Hosea is being fulfilled in the presence of the guests (Jesus' disciples), who should be, and are, rejoicing and not fasting.

The Pharisees and the disciples of John fasted because they were longing for the day when God would again show his favour to Israel. They were in mourning, waiting for the day when God would restore Israel because they didn't believe that God's promise had yet been fulfilled. Jesus declares that with his coming that day had now arrived. But Jesus also says that days are coming when his disciples will fast. Those days are when their bridegroom is taken from the guests. The early church understood this to refer to the time after Jesus ascended into heaven and before he returns to earth again – his second coming (Acts 13:3; 14:23; 27:9). Today is therefore a time for fasting, but not religiously like the Pharisees and disciples of John. Instead, we are to fast as those who know that the bridegroom had once come to earth and who long for his return. Somehow, we are now able to both rejoice in our relationship with Jesus and to fast in obedience to Jesus' instructions, whilst we patiently wait (Matt. 9:15).

Jesus now continues and gives us two more illustrations of the radical difference between the old and new covenants.

In Jesus' second answer, he speaks about patching up old clothes with a new piece of cloth. The old clothes have already shrunk and become worn during their natural use. The new patch is stronger, more taught and fresher. If someone makes holes in the already weaker old garment by sewing in the new patch, it is weakened further still. As natural use of the garment then continues, the new patch will then itself shrink and pull making the tear worsen. The new is so different that the old cannot cope with it (Matt. 9:16).

My mother, Sylvia, worked for many years in the same manufacturing factory where I served my aircraft engineering apprenticeship; she was a professional seamstress. She would machine sew through thick webbing and industrial-strength material that is used on an ejector seat, and in the harness for the parachute. Even these super-strong materials had a shelf life and after a period of time, they would be replaced even if they had never been used. Why? Because it had aged and become old, and in the production of life-saving ejector seats no short cut is taken – the old is replaced with the new.

In Jesus' third answer, he speaks about pouring new wine into old wineskins. New skins are flexible and can stretch but will eventually become more brittle with age. Old wineskins have stretched already and become weaker and brittle. As new wine continues to ferment, the pressure of new wine in this process would expand and therefore burst if inside the old brittle skins. Both the wine and the wineskin would be ruined. The new wine of the Kingdom could not be preserved in the parched and brittle skin of the old religious legalism.

The initial question about fasting assumed that Jesus' teaching and ministry was only a slight alteration or a patch upon the existing system of Judaism. Jesus, however, informs them that fasting is different for his disciples precisely because with his coming into the world something completely new has begun. You cannot just pour the content of the new covenant into the frame of the old covenant. Jesus needs to perform some heart surgery within people, so that the truest and purest form of the old law could be made known. He did not come to put a new coat of paint on an old building, but rather to begin a new movement starting within Judaism – if only they would accept it (Matt. 9:17).

In Conclusion

What are the applications for us today? We fast because we live between the two eras of Jesus on planet earth. We fast because we believe that the King is our bridegroom who has come to inaugurate his Kingdom, and we very eagerly anticipate his return to consummate that same Kingdom. When we fast, we aim to hear God's voice and to live out the desires of our heavenly Father's heart.

Fasting hurts – it is costly! Just try the easiest form and you will soon understand. Please be led by the Holy Spirit in obeying his instruction of when and how to fast, and make sure from a practical and health point of view that you are not attempting something dangerous. For example, check with a doctor or nutritionist first if you are diabetic.

Jesus teaches his disciples how to fast and indicates they should do so after he is gone. After the early church is formed, Jesus' disciples began to fast two days per week, but on different days so that they were not confused or associated with the fasting of the Pharisees. This is sometimes still done today. If God is asking this of you be careful that the regular nature or rhythm never becomes just a religious activity. At the same time though, as Jesus' disciples today, we should fast, and not excuse ourselves by thinking that it is just a religious thing and not relational with God. On the contrary, it should be deeply relational. Fasting helps align our body and soul with our spirit within, and therefore facilitates the possibility of an even greater connection with the Holy Spirit, as we attune ourselves to him. We benefit in intimacy with God and become much more spiritually alert in a spiritual Kingdom.

So, when did you last fast? When do you plan to fast next? Are you listening to the Holy Spirit's prompting in this regard? It is a high price that disciples are willing to pay.

CHAPTER FIVE

Citizens Are Authorised to Demonstrate

Next Jesus raises a dead girl back to life and, on the way to doing so, he heals a woman sick with an impossible-to-fix bleeding (Matt. 9:18-26). Surely, he can do nothing more to demonstrate his deity and the power of his Kingdom. News about Jesus was spreading fast throughout the region, when he goes on to heal two blind men by his touch and delivers a man who was mute because of demonic possession. These kinds of demonstrations were things that had never been seen before... *"The crowd was amazed and said, 'Nothing like this has ever been seen in Israel'"* (Matt. 9:27-33).

Jesus continues preaching the Kingdom and heals every disease and illness, even though he is accused of being demonic himself by the religious leaders (Matt. 9:34-36). He simply ignores them and gets on with healing everyone who comes to him of every ailment that they have – just incredible! Why do you think he demonstrated this new Kingdom and its power so much? It is because he was about to send out his disciples into the mission field as workers in this new Kingdom. Has Jesus changed? Has the Kingdom changed? Are we the disciples of Jesus today? If these things have not changed then why are we often not going out into the mission field and demonstrating our King's Kingdom in all its power? We are to imitate Jesus in everything we do and in how we conduct ourselves. We adopt both his agenda and his methods. These methods are helpfully described by Miller as... "*Spirit anointed proclamation and Spirit empowered demonstration*".[32]

Pray for Workers

"*Then he said to his disciples, 'The harvest is plentiful but the workers are few. Ask the Lord of the harvest, therefore, to send out workers into his harvest field'*" (Matt. 9:37-38).

Jesus says to his disciples that there is a plentiful harvest of souls. Jesus knows everything, so there are those waiting to hear. Many in fact are willing to hear about the Kingdom, to see a demonstration of the Kingdom, to follow Jesus. If only there were enough messengers to proclaim and demonstrate it. The workers need to be multiplied. You see, in view of the cost of being a disciple, Jesus is aware that not many will truly serve him or work for him. Disciples must be willing to be workers for the Kingdom – a disciple of Jesus cannot simply go to church on Sunday.

Jesus says that we are to pray that God – who is the Lord of the harvest – will send out workers into his harvest field. Have you been asking God this question or petitioning him to send out workers?

Be the Answer

"*Jesus called his twelve disciples to him and gave them authority to **drive out impure spirits and to heal every disease and***

---

[32] Miller, D. *The Kingdom and the Power. The Kingdom of God: A Pentecostal Interpretation* (Springfield: AIA Publications, 2008), P33-4.

illness. *² These are the names of the twelve apostles: first, Simon (who is called Peter) and his brother Andrew; James son of Zebedee, and his brother John; ³ Philip and Bartholomew; Thomas and Matthew the tax collector; James son of Alphaeus, and Thaddaeus; ⁴ Simon the Zealot and Judas Iscariot, who betrayed him. ⁵ These twelve Jesus sent out with the following instructions: 'Do not go among the Gentiles or enter any town of the Samaritans. ⁶ Go rather to the lost sheep of Israel. ⁷ As you go, proclaim this message: "The kingdom of heaven has come near." ⁸* **Heal those who are ill, raise the dead, cleanse those who have leprosy, drive out demons.** *Freely you have received; freely give"* (Matt. 10:1-8).

After Jesus has told the disciples to pray for workers, he calls them to him again and now sends them out as workers. They are the answer to their own prayers. Some say, be careful what you pray for! But I want us to take seriously this request of Jesus and to prayerfully consider our role in being the answer to this prayer, that we are supposed to pray.

Before Jesus sends them out, he makes sure that the disciples know that they are equipped and authorised to represent the King, as they proclaim and demonstrate the Kingdom. He gives them authority to drive out impure spirits and to heal every disease and illness. You and I have this authority today, to drive out any impure spirit and to heal every disease and illness, because we go in his name, with his power and with his authority. Do you realise that it's not only when we gather together, but particularly when we leave our church buildings and go out, that we are authorised as representatives of the Kingdom? To make this clear, that it is personal and individual, the disciples are named one after another. Not one is missed out. We cannot, therefore, pass on this responsibility to other 'more mature' disciples, or those with the five-fold ministry gift of evangelism. **It is for all of us to replicate the ministry and the teachings of Jesus**. We also see that all were included in the upper room when the Holy Spirit was poured out on all flesh, men and women of all ages (Acts 1:8; 2:17-18). It was at Pentecost that the power of the Kingdom was fully transferred to all of Jesus' disciples, and the same Spirit that empowered him now empowers us.[33]

Our Instructions

The disciples were sent with some instructions. They were told at this point to go only to people who were Jewish. That was the focus of Jesus' own ministry, with few exceptions. For now, Jesus wants a clear initial focus for how the extension of his Kingdom is to advance. Why is the instruction only to go to the lost sheep of Israel and bypass the Gentiles and Samaritans? Remember Matthew is writing to Jewish Christians who need help to know how to live out their lives as disciples in this new Kingdom. That is their starting point: local mission to their own people group. We know elsewhere that Jesus says to go to Jerusalem, Judea, Samaria and to the end of the earth (Acts 1:8, 8:1). Jesus emphasises the starting point for those disciples two thousand years ago, but it's not that this was to be the only place to go to for all of history. Jesus also tells them that they should travel light and be dependent upon the hospitality of those they go to minister to.

---

[33] Miller, D. *The Kingdom and the Power*, P112.

Jesus says that the disciples are to proclaim the very same message as John the Baptist and Jesus' own message... "*The kingdom of heaven has come near*". It is identical. I believe Jesus knew of a topic that would forever cause people to think and consider – heaven. They were to proclaim this message, then demonstrate it, to show people exactly what it meant. If I went to someone and said "heaven is here" – they would most likely respond – "Ok show me; I'd like to see that", or perhaps, "I don't believe you unless you can prove it", or even, "where do you mean exactly, show me". You see, the Kingdom of heaven is upon you... "*The Spirit of the Lord is on me, because he has anointed me to proclaim good news to the poor. He has sent me to proclaim freedom for the prisoners and recovery of sight for the blind, to set the oppressed free*" (Luke 4:18). It is everywhere across this earth and yet it breaks in as you go as an authorised representative, and where you proclaim and demonstrate it in moments of *Kairos* (an opportune time for action) that clearly evidence it. That takes courage and boldness and it requires faith because you say it is here and then have to rely on God to back up your claim. Can you think of a reason why he would not want to back up what he has asked us to do? If we are to go out as the workers into the harvest field today and proclaim the same message, it means we go out and talk about heaven and the King of heaven. We tell people it is near or right here, expecting then to be the answer, through the power of the Holy Spirit at work within us, to meet their need.

Now the 'rubber hits the road'. Jesus repeats from verse one that we are to heal those who are ill and to drive out demons (completely nullifying the influence and presence of demons in a person or place), so these things should be part of our spiritual 'staple diet' as disciples. We need to learn from scripture, and from others with more experience than us, how to minister these effectively. Now though, Jesus ups the ante adding that we are also to cleanse the leper (an incurable disease of that time in history) and to raise the dead. Yet many disciples of Jesus today are struggling with understanding healing and exorcism for themselves, let alone be able to demonstrate physical and spiritual healing. Perhaps many are confused or even afraid to try them. How then are we supposed to progress into healing incurable diseases or raising the dead?

Firstly, we have to remember that in Matthew's account Jesus has literally just demonstrated all these things to his disciples; they have seen what to do and how to do them, so they should **believe and have faith**. Secondly, disciples today should still desire to do these things because Jesus is the same yesterday, today and forever; so our making of other disciples should certainly include these as part of their basic training.

By God's grace, we have seen people healed and on occasions have cast out demons in the church I lead (we have seen the same on mission trips overseas as well). That is not the case for many churches in the UK. Sadly, many believers in Jesus have never seen or been part of such things. They are not 'in the programme' or 'on the agenda' for discipleship training. But if we think we are doing ok as a church, then we need to think again, because we are still not seeing all that Jesus sent us out to do. I would imagine though, that few churches here have seen incurable diseases cured, and fewer still will have seen the dead raised. What about in your nation, your denomination, your church or in your life? Jesus sends all of his disciples out with this purpose and does not delineate between such things (Matt. 10:5-7).

I would just like to add, that we can show the love of God in many ways and with practical and social helps too. These are not to be left out and are needed to help feed the hungry or fix up a garden for an elderly neighbour, as examples. There does seem to be a leaning towards this type of outworking of our faith. These are incredible doors into people's lives and we should be living this way. However, I do sense a lagging behind in the demonstration of the spiritual Kingdom that Jesus ushered in. So here I'm just wanting to highlight and encourage citizens of the Kingdom, to see that they are supposed to do both.

It's Free to Receive and Give

We all love getting something for free. The 'buy one get one free' signs at any shopping mall certainly grab our attention. It costs us nothing to become part of the Kingdom of Heaven. It costs us nothing to have our sins forgiven. It costs us nothing to have eternity with a loving God. Salvation is free! We gained so much without cost on our behalf. It truly is amazing grace that accomplished this for us. We have great encouragement from Jesus, knowing that he gave these most astonishing extras away for free. He never once thought to charge a fee or to take up an offering!

As the disciples who make up the church, we have received so much from God, but non-believers also benefit because his goodness falls upon both the righteous and the unrighteous (Matt. 5:45). This does seem to be the case for the healings that

I have been privileged to experience being a part of. I'd say probably half were for believers and half were not. God has lavished his generosity and kindness upon mankind. He even gifts the Holy Spirit to live within his disciples, to help us and come alongside us, as we go and demonstrate the Kingdom in an equally lavish way. We are empowered to do this... *"Freely you have received; freely give"* (Matt. 10:8).

The Indispensable Holy Spirit

Making disciples is teaching people to walk in the Spirit, to love their neighbour as themselves, to use the gifts of the Spirit (spiritual gifts), and to grow in the fruit (singular) of the Spirit, all nine of them (Gal. 5:13-26). If you live in and walk with the Spirit, fruit will be the result.

The Spirit leads us; he does not make either a bunch of rules to follow (legalism) or leave us no rules at all (licence to sin). Instead, he gently leads us into all righteousness by convicting our hearts. Ladd says that... *"the righteousness of God's Kingdom is the product of God's reign in the human heart"*,[34] and so we must be willing. This is exactly what Jesus is all about: transforming the hearts of people that are willing. This helps us to be better able to enjoy living in the Kingdom of Heaven now. We then have to choose to submit our will to his. It is the Spirit who forms the character of Jesus inside us. This is what we mean if we ask Jesus to 'come into our hearts'; we are asking to receive the Spirit, who perfectly as God,

---

[34] Ladd, G. E. *The Gospel of the Kingdom. Popular Expositions on the Kingdom of God* (Grand Rapids: William B. Eerdmans Publishing Company, 1974), P83.

represents Jesus within us. The Father did send Jesus to us on earth, but has now, since his ascension, received him back. It is the Spirit who now takes the role of God's ministry on this earth.

We believe in Jesus and we receive the Spirit of Jesus (John 20:22 Acts 8:15, 17). This is the one and the same Holy Spirit. Paul was concerned that the believers in Ephesus had received the Holy Spirit... "*Did you receive the Holy Spirit when you believed?*" (Acts 19:2). Jesus also said... "*But if it is by the Spirit of God that I drive out demons, then the kingdom of God has come upon you*" (Matt. 12:28). The Spirit helped Jesus in his ministry and continues to help us today. Do you notice though, that there does appear to be a lack of Kingdom demonstration and power today, especially among many Western and first world believers who reject baptism in the Spirit because all believers receive the Spirit? They perhaps don't expect to operate in the Spirit or they hold back from doing so, possibly through fear. However, we know that the Kingdom cannot exclude the Holy Spirit (Rom 14:17) and that the same Spirit lives within us... "*Do you not know that your bodies are temples of the Holy Spirit, who is in you, whom you have received from God?*" (1 Cor. 6:19). Therefore, we must learn to operate in the use of spiritual gifts. As we learn to walk in step with the Spirit and get to know him, then Kingdom language and behaviour will become ours, because discovering the Spirit is precisely the way in which we discover how to operate in the Kingdom. He may ask us to go to places and to do things we could never have imagined.

It was during a mission trip to India, at the end of a long day and a long evening church gathering, with the team tired, hungry and ready for dinner, that as we were getting ready to leave, our host asked if we could go as a team and pray for one more person. We agreed, a little reluctantly myself if I'm really honest, and we were taken into a small side room. There we found a paralytic lying man on a makeshift type camping bed, having been carried in by friends. Reminded immediately of that Bible account when a paralytic is lowered through the roof of a house so that Jesus could heal him, my attitude changed instantly and we all began to worship and pray over this man. He was in his thirties, had a medical background and had fallen from a third-floor height and broken his neck. After twenty minutes or so he was able, for the first time, to feel his feet and slightly move his toes. We continued for another ten minutes, but that was the condition we left him in. We were encouraged that he had feeling in his feet for the first time since the accident, but also disappointed not to have seen a healing of Biblical proportions. This was a Thursday evening, if I recall correctly. As a team, we moved on the next day and were busy with ministry over the weekend at a wedding and also a church service. Monday turned into a very long day travelling in a cramped car. It was hot, noisy through incessant use of the car horns in Indian culture, and after eight to ten hours on the road it was dark and we were getting hungry. Our driver was almost falling asleep, and was replaced at the wheel by our same host, who then received a phone call. He told us that the paralytic man had on Sunday walked himself into church. We rejoiced! The lesson I learnt that day was that it is the Holy Spirit who does the healing. By this time we were hundreds of miles away, so he ensured that Jesus got the glory. We just had to be courageous and willing to do all that we could do, to bring about a Kingdom demonstration that had presented itself to us. It is something I will never forget.

It is the Spirit who does these things; our job as disciples is to be the obedient and willing vessels through which he normally chooses to act. This means knowing the authority we have and exercising our faith in Jesus, carrying these out as we go. This won't always be easy for us to do, as we can very quickly get out of step with the Spirit by walking in the flesh, or in ignorance, or even in disobedience. Let's instead do our very best to keep in step with the wonderful Spirit. It is possible!

Koinonia – working together and with God

To make a disciple is to produce someone capable of doing everything that Jesus commands as our King. We will need others who also walk with the Spirit to help us, and we should avoid doing this journeying on our own. I am not saying that we should become dependent upon others to always carry us, as there will be times when we alone are faced with a situation and have to individually walk in step with the Spirit. On the other hand, walking with others who also walk in the Spirit will help us to remain accountable and to continue learning by allowing others to speak into our lives and therefore to keep us growing.

Isn't it strange how God often takes people from different races, backgrounds, cultures and temperaments, throws them into a room (called a church), and expects them to live in harmony? But that is precisely what he wants and expects. This is the *koinonia*, the Greek word for fellowship that the Spirit brings and builds amongst us. It is beautiful, loving and harmonious. In this community environment that the Spirit facilitates, we are all to remain loyal citizens or subjects to just one, Jesus our King. We don't follow Paul, Apollos or Cephas (1 Cor. 1:12). In other words we don't follow people, because if we do then we are still worldly, walking out of step with the Spirit... *"For since there is jealousy and quarrelling among you, are you not worldly? Are you not acting like mere humans? ⁴ For when one says, "I follow Paul," and another, "I follow Apollos," are you not mere human beings?"* (1 Cor. 3:3-4). Paul explains exactly who people are, even great ones, who walk in step with the Spirit... *"For we are co-workers in God's service; you are God's field, God's building"* (1 Cor. 3:9). Follow the Spirit and he will grow and build you and lead you into all truth (John 16:13). Doing so in a Spirit-filled community is extremely helpful. This type of *koinonia* is a prophetic community, which must therefore be led by leaders who are themselves led by the Spirit... *"May the grace of the Lord Jesus Christ, and the love of God, and the fellowship of the Holy Spirit be with you all"* (2 Cor. 13:14).

In Conclusion

Will we say yes to being the answer to our own prayers? Will we go with our simple instructions and work in the harvest field? What we have freely received we must freely give away. What Jesus expects of us is that we simply do what he did. We are as Christians, supposed to be 'little-Christs' after all.

Disciples being sent out today will greatly benefit if they have been baptised in the Holy Spirit; they would not be able to demonstrate the Kingdom in power otherwise. We can and should, all do good works (or a social type gospel), but we must also demonstrate the spiritual power of the Kingdom. The Spirit gifts us and grows us, helping us to be good subjects that do the will of the King. We cannot do this without the Holy Spirit, who is certainly worth getting to know. He guides and leads us on the most incredible adventure, where we will actually get to witness the things we read about in the Bible.

God establishes and extends the influence of his Kingdom through people who are led by the Spirit, which is our most important qualification. Without experiencing life in the Kingdom, we would be like blind guides – how can a person possibly show others the way? The way we accomplish this is through building a colonial base on earth for our King to return to (one day), a place where he can unsaddle and tie his white horse. Be bold and courageous, therefore, in the knowledge that you are authorised to demonstrate the Kingdom of Heaven on this earth. You are a citizen after all.

CHAPTER SIX

Citizens Have Total Commitment

All in? That was the title of a message that challenged one of my best friends Kevin and changed the direction of his life. He was a committed churchgoer and someone who was doing all the right Christian things: active in church, running a business with Christian principles, doing his best to be the best husband he could and raising a family to follow Jesus. Money was coming in and he was living the American dream as well as the Christian dream. Kevin had shared how those two simple words struck such a chord in his heart that he became willing to leave that life and be obedient to his calling to serve Jesus in England. God had connected us as friends, and then on a short-term mission trip as well. As soon as he knew that I was heading to Broadstairs to pastor a church[35] on the south-east coast, he and his wife Tracey came to visit. I moved there in July 2015 and they were with me visiting in August. By December, after getting through all the rather complicated arrangements to move a family of five from Texas to England, they had landed. What was it that best described this wonderful family, with all the change, all the risk...and yet all the adventure? I think that the title of this chapter would do nicely.

Please don't think that following the call of Jesus will mean that life is going to be plain sailing. Things weren't perfect, they

---

[35] www.elimoasischurch.com

never are, but we grew a deep friendship, and at our very core we were totally for each other, supporting and encouraging in so many ways. Kevin knew how to serve and he knew how to be a servant too. He never went against my leadership but supported me all the way. Three years after that very first visit, in August 2018, I was at Budapest Airport boarding my short flight back to the UK, after a brief trip to missionary friends in Hungary. Kevin phoned. It was leukaemia. Everyone in our church family was stunned and we immediately began to pray. We prayed like never before. As did many across the world that knew him. Kevin did all he could to ensure that his family were going to be ok, then he entered into a ten-day intensive course of chemotherapy. As he began his treatment, he asked the nursing staff who the really sick people were, so that he could pray for them. He always put the needs of others ahead of his own. I visited him after my day's work on day nine of his treatment, which was on a Monday evening. He was in fine spirits, even hoping to be released by the weekend. We spoke excitedly about this Kingdom Perspective Series and he offered to help me in any way that he could. Wednesday things went downhill as his body began to react negatively to the intense treatment. By Thursday evening, he was moved into the Intensive Care Unit (ICU). He was placed in a coma and onto a ventilator. Three weeks later he was promoted to glory. Kevin was only forty-seven. He continues to set the best example to our church of what it truly means to be 'all in'. It wasn't plain sailing and remains that way for the McManus family, who are often in my thoughts and prayers.

At the beginning of Matthew chapter ten, Jesus commissions and sends out the twelve disciples on their first-ever mission trip. They have been authorised to demonstrate the Kingdom on behalf of its King, just as Jesus had taught them. Their training had been intense and shown them the incredible and diverse ways in which Jesus would minister. They are sent, and interestingly Jesus does not go with them. They are left to their own devices, expected to heal the sick, cast out demons, cure the incurable and raise the dead, freely giving away what they had freely received.

Less is More

"Do not get any gold or silver or copper to take with you in your belts – no bag for the journey or extra shirt or sandals or a staff, for the worker is worth his keep. Whatever town or village you enter, search there for some worthy person and stay at their house until you leave. As you enter the home, give it your greeting. If the home is deserving, let your peace rest on it; if it is not, let your peace return to you. If anyone will not welcome you or listen to your words, leave that home or town and shake the dust off your feet. Truly I tell you, it will be more bearable for Sodom and Gomorrah on the Day of Judgment than for that town" (Matt. 10:9-15).

If we go out anywhere what is the first thing we do? We check for our phones, handbags, wallets and our keys – and that's just to pop out to see a neighbour or buy some milk. What happens if we stay overnight somewhere? Well, we would need a decent overnight bag. For a short holiday, it's probably a medium-sized suitcase. For a longer holiday, it's a case large enough for the kitchen sink! We pack and take so many things with us, just in case. We do like to be prepared.

Imagine this scene, you are in your local church setting and Jesus walks in. He teaches you something about his Kingdom and then he shows you how to demonstrate it. Then he says "I authorise you now to go", and he sends you out of your church building or meeting place to go and get on with sharing and demonstrating the things of heaven. After the initial shock, you pick up your coat, keys, mobile, wallet, handbag, backpack and anything else you arrived with, and Jesus shouts: "Stop! No money, no items to trade with, no bag, no extra coat, no phone, no make-up, no car – leave it all behind". Could you do it? Could you trust God completely to provide as you go?

Hospitality to God's messengers was seen as a sacred duty in Israel, from the time of Abraham and Sarah cooking for the angels of the Lord (Gen. 18:4-8), right through to the disciples on the road to Emmaus (Luke 24:29). Those who were given gifts to bring from the heavenly realm would have been taken care of by those who had just received from God for free, perhaps their healing or miracle. Doing so would have been the recipient's delight and something unthinkable not to do. They would have freely and most joyfully taken care of the heavenly messenger's needs. What this means is that the Kingdom of Heaven had to be demonstrated and made real to those who had not seen it before, otherwise no one would feel they had to take care of their needs. Things suddenly get a bit more real now. No life-changing demonstration, combined with no money or items to trade with and they would have no dinner or bed for the night. Therefore, **a citizen of the Kingdom of Heaven has to be able to make the Kingdom become a very real thing for those who need to experience it**.

If we take nothing or have less, then we have to be dependent on the Holy Spirit working in power through us. This enables us to provide more for others; rather than giving someone a little money, we give them a healing touch from heaven. I do wonder if we are more dependent upon our own provision or on the Spirit's power. I believe that if we live more simply and with fewer material items, then we will be more focused on the power of God, in and through us, than being distracted by things. Less is definitely more. Perhaps there are some things that you have suddenly realised you need to give up.

Also in these verses, we find the often-used statement '*the labourer deserves his food*' (ESV), or '*the worker is worth his keep*' (NIV). Frequently used to say that a Pastor or church worker should get a salary. I think the more accurate context here is disciples of Jesus going on their first mission trip without him, and with absolutely nothing material – just a big helping of faith! They have been authorised, given their metaphorical Kingdom of Heaven ID cards, and are instructed to demonstrate the Kingdom. That's it. Jesus has not said to work in the fields for the day so they you can earn some money to buy food. If we seek first the Kingdom and demonstrate it as we go, then God will take care of our needs, perhaps miraculously or simply through the help of those to whom we have brought a slice of heaven (Matt. 10:9-10).

A Person of Peace

If we find the right place to stay, there should then be no need to change our lodgings. Mission is not about staying at the nicest hotel. It is about staying with the one that is a worthy person. That worthiness will be evidenced by their glad acceptance of the message of the Kingdom of Heaven that we proclaim. Often this type of person is known as a 'person of peace'. They will be gratefully hospitable and also facilitators for Kingdom work in that city, town or village. They will have connections that will help the mission (Matt. 10:11).

We should accept the hospitality shown to us. Sometimes this may not be as easy as it seems. Once I was in a poverty-stricken Roman Gypsy family home in Macedonia, they had used all they could to provide some food for our team as their guests. It tasted dreadful, so what do you do? Yes, you remain grateful, chew with a smile and then swallow.

Carriers of Peace

We are to give our host family, and their house, our greeting. In England, we would turn up and expect a nice cup of tea. Well, there is a little more to it than that. You see we carry the Spirit of God within us, and so we have the ability to give heavenly greetings of God's peace to people and their homes. A common Jewish practice of hospitality was to literally pour oil as a token of honour on your guests. We carry the heavenly oil, the Holy Spirit, and are able to offer him. This offer of peace is extremely significant; it is what the world is longing for and we have it to offer for free. We should never underestimate what we carry and the one we represent. Remember that Jesus is the ultimate Prince of Peace (Isa. 9:6).

Those that reject our Kingdom offer are not worthy of us as its messengers. Jesus says that if the offer is not received, then withdraw it, 'shaking off' the unholy dust as you leave. We are only human and might feel rejected as we attempt to deliver the message of the Kingdom, but it is Jesus who is the one that is being rejected. We don't have to take it so personally. Yet there is a severity to the action of rejecting Jesus that is highlighted by this symbolic action. We though are not to react poorly. Did you notice that this even applies to a town? Jesus essentially did the same of his own home town, Nazareth. If God sends us as disciples into a new town or village to declare the Kingdom and begin making disciples in that place (usually called a church plant or a missional/gospel community), we should realise the wider offer of peace that we take and hopefully we won't have to withdraw (Matt. 10:12-14).

Not our Judgement

The rejection of Jesus is a severe thing indeed. Sodom and Gomorrah are the famous two cities that were judged and instantly burnt up with such severity that there were no survivors. It was due to their longstanding and shameful ways, which were clearly demonstrated in the actions they intended to take towards God's servants. It is an even greater judgement that awaits those who reject Jesus, perhaps because they have either seen him directly or have had a demonstration of his Kingdom through his disciples, in a way that the people of these OT cities did not. I guess it was at least over quickly.

Rejecting Jesus is the total opposite of what he requires in being totally committed to him. A final day of judgement does await all created beings, both human and angelic. However, this judgement belongs to the Lord (Rom. 12:19), not you or I, and it will be an eternal one (Matt. 10:15).

Reasons to Commit

We know the privileged position that we hold as citizens of the Kingdom, but this will require our total commitment. Why should we commit in this way, won't that mess up or even ruin our lives? The Kingdom is only at hand or available because Jesus is. He was and still is totally committed to us. As we grow to become more and more like him, surely his ways should naturally, yes even supernaturally, become our ways. This is the kind of citizens that he is looking for.

Jesus was in complete control of every situation that he found himself in, whether storms, the demonic or even the dead. He is King over everything but refused to be crowned as one from an earthly perspective. Israel at one point wanted to make Jesus King by force, to lead them out from the hand of their Roman oppressors (John 6:15). But Jesus was looking for true citizens as willing subjects, who were few indeed, despite the fact that this is the basic and foundational demand of the Kingdom: man's will yielded to that of their King.[36] We could be made king, president, prime minister etc. over our nation, but if our citizens will not obey us we are not ruling after all. Jesus is the King of a supernatural Kingdom, not an earthly one, and he chose a crown of thorns instead. Throughout history since Jesus walked this earth, many people including some so-called disciples, have wanted to get what they can from the King – a blessing, a healing or worldly riches – but they refuse to be his willing and committed subjects.[37]

---

[36] Ladd, G. E. *The Gospel of the Kingdom*, P97.

[37] Pawson, D. *Kingdoms in Conflict* (Reading: Anchor Recordings Ltd., 2015).

I am a citizen by right of the United Kingdom, but if I refuse to follow its laws then I could well end up detained in one of Her Majesty's prisons. That would make me an unwilling subject even though I am still a citizen – albeit with my rights and privileges removed for a time period. How many citizens of the Kingdom today still find themselves locked up in so many ways due to anger, bitterness, control issues, unforgiveness and even addictions? All because they refuse to be totally committed to Jesus.

In Conclusion

We show that we are totally committed when we learn to fully rely on the Spirit, as we go and demonstrate that the Kingdom of heaven has come near. We work with people of peace and leave with them what we carry, our heavenly peace. We leave all judgment about everything to God. Jesus is totally committed to us and we should be totally committed to him. He has defined the requirements of his citizens in terms of behaviour (Matt. 5-7) and discipleship (Matt. 8-10). This is what we are to be totally committed to as we walk in the Spirit.

We are now halfway through this section, the making of a disciple. I wonder if you sense that the true cost of citizenship is beginning to mount up. We have seen that this means many things: being convinced, willing and available (Matt. 4:18-22); enthusiastic and without hesitation (Matt. 8:18-22); obedient and merciful (Matt. 9:9-13); having regular fasts (Matt. 9:14-17); going as authorised workers and demonstrators of heaven (Matt. 9:37-10:8); and being totally committed to Jesus (Matt. 10:9-15).

Remember, salvation is free but discipleship will cost you your life. Are you *all in?*

CHAPTER SEVEN

Citizens Expect Opposition

One of the hardest moments of that mission trip to India, where we had rejoiced over the paralytic being healed, came during a visit to a real-life village for outcasts. Who knew that these places even existed? The homes were like old small sheds somehow managing to stay upright; sanitation and hygiene were deplorable. The people that had been sent to live there included those deformed by leprosy, the blind, the cripples, the mentally unstable – I guess you get the picture. I've never seen such a place. It was remote and away from towns and villages, which is saying something in a country with the world's largest population; people seem to be everywhere. Except here. We took in food and some medical supplies as we had some nurses serving on our team. The villagers all came into the main meeting house on the site for food, blankets, physical health checks being made by our nurses, and then spiritual health checks as the rest of the team prayed for almost the whole camp. We had watched one man with no legs drag himself up to the meeting house. He did not complain and simply smiled and refused any offer of help.

We did all we could that day. The gospel was preached, we worshipped and we prayed for hours, as well as all the practical elements. Now I would love to tell you that we saw miracle after miracle. The reality though, was that we saw only a few instant healings, which would normally have us jumping with joy. Yet in this place, we left feeling like we had been through a spiritual battle zone and not seen anywhere near the level, or the amount, of things that we had hoped for. We did our best. I sensed though, that God had done more than we could only see externally, and knew he had been working on healing hearts as well, which in the bigger scheme of things is where true freedom is found. We left our peace there.

None of us likes to suffer or even to see others suffering, but it's a fact of life in the fallen world in which we live. Often one person's gain is another person's pain. What ways do you suffer in this life? Perhaps it's in the area of ill-health, be that physical, emotional, mental or spiritual, or in finances or even in just walking with others, loved ones and friends, who are going through difficult and traumatic times. Turn on any of the news channels and you will see suffering of every type happening all over this world. We will now see that mission for Jesus will also at times mean suffering.

Warning and Encouragement

"I am sending you out like sheep among wolves. Therefore be as shrewd as snakes and as innocent as doves. ¹⁷ Be on your guard; you will be handed over to the local councils and be flogged in the synagogues. ¹⁸ On my account you will be brought before governors and kings as witnesses to them and to the Gentiles. ¹⁹ But when they arrest you, do not worry about what to say or how to say it. At that time you will be given what to say, ²⁰ for it will not be you speaking, but the Spirit of your Father speaking through you" (Matt. 10:16-20).

Notice again that citizens are a sent people who must not just remain inside the walls of their respective church. Jesus sends out his disciples but with some warnings about what to expect, in the form of the coming opposition. It will be nasty 'out there' at times, which will equate to suffering. As disciples of Jesus, we are in a battle, whether we prefer to acknowledge it or not. This battle is in the spiritual realm; it is not against flesh and blood (Eph. 6:12). We fight with the weapons of fasting and prayer, with an urgency and with fervent passion. If you join any national army the first thing you are given is a uniform to identify you as a soldier. The same is true of becoming a disciple of Jesus; we join an army except without a visible uniform to identify us. This can have the disadvantage of us not always taking our spiritual duty seriously. We are to be wise and innocent of evil in our own lives as well as being on guard, because the enemy is still able to identify us.

Jesus told his disciples that opportunities to witness would come and so would persecution from the law courts and civil rulers, that would result in public flogging (severe physical beating). Jesus would later experience this himself, just before his crucifixion. Flogging was literal and physical in Jesus' day, and is still literal and physical for millions of persecuted Christians around the world today, but for the majority of us, it is neither literal nor physical. That does not mean that we don't suffer, because we do, but the means of that suffering may differ. Spiritual attack and demonic oppression are not nice but will follow citizens of the Kingdom that move forward and take ground. I notice these often and have come to realise that if I am not experiencing some form spiritual resistance, then either I or my church have stopped moving forwards. Perhaps it is only more of an internal suffering in sickness or depression, unless Jesus sends us to places where it is far more dangerous to be a disciple. I know some people, who have been attacked and beaten when on an overseas mission trip, and one of them was stabbed multiple times and blinded in one eye. They had just been discussing spiritual warfare whilst walking back to their accommodation at night, when this unprovoked attack took place. Persecution will always bring opportunity for further testimony about the goodness of Jesus and his Kingdom, and this attack became a very real testimony to the goodness of God. Opponents will actively pursue you because that is what all opponents do. The Devil and his demons are our enemies. But we are not to fear them and we are to walk in purity and be wise as we engage in battle. This does not mean only for an hour per week at the church prayer meeting, if we have not forgotten to write that into our busy schedules, but being on guard or spiritually alert moment by moment each day.

We have the Holy Spirit with us during these times and if we let him, he will even speak through us, in the difficult and challenging circumstances that we come up against. We can take comfort that we do not need to worry about what to say as we trust in this promise of Jesus. We don't have to figure things out but just trust that our heavenly Father will not abandon us or ever let us down. Up to this point in Matthew's Gospel the Spirit is mentioned with Jesus and his Kingdom (Matt. 1:18, 20; 3:11, 16; 4:1), now the phrase, "*the Spirit of your Father*", shows us that both Father and Son speak to and through us, via the Spirit, who gives us the words to speak.

During the first overseas mission trip that my church took to Estonia, we used the simple concept of keeping our spiritual antenna up! A bit like the first black and white portable televisions that came out and had their own antennae. If the antenna was not correctly positioned the screen became completely fuzzy. Similarly, if we are not attuned to the Holy Spirit, we will struggle to bring the spiritual Kingdom of Heaven to others.

Jesus, the most hated?

"Brother will betray brother to death, and a father his child; children will rebel against their parents and have them put to death. 22 You will be hated by everyone because of me, but the one who stands firm to the end will be saved. 23 When you are persecuted in one place, flee to another. Truly I tell you, you will not finish going through the towns of Israel before the Son of Man comes" (Matt. 10:21-23).

Until people understand and accept Jesus, they might be very indifferent about him, but many hate him. I would say that Jesus is probably the most hated person that has ever lived. Now, whether you love him or hate him, this world simply will never be able to ignore him. He will continue to divide people by their opinions, which in extreme cases may even lead to unthinkable family betrayal. Not many of us will have everyone in our family and closest relationships following Jesus. Even the closest family can end up at odds with one another because of Jesus – even to the point of killing each other. That may sound far-fetched in the modern Western world, but it does happen. Don't forget those in other parts of the world who are ostracised from their entire extended family, because they think that they have been betrayed by the one who has chosen to follow Jesus. This can lead to an 'honour killing', a religiously permitted murder.

When we become citizens of the Kingdom our allegiance changes to Jesus. We still love our family and our nation, but nothing comes before our relationship with Jesus Christ. Being fiercely patriotic is still allowed; some countries like the USA require you to pledge allegiance to their flag. We all do this in some way even if just at sporting events, like the World Cup or the Olympics. We can be very patriotic, serve our country and cheer for our national team, as long as that is not ahead of a disciple's primary allegiance to Jesus.

Endurance and perseverance are key for us as disciples. Jesus says encouragingly that he will return and until he does, his mission continues through his citizens. Even if we have to flee for our safety at times, we are to keep going.

Reasons not to fear Persecution

"The student is not above the teacher, nor a servant above his master.[25] It is enough for students to be like their teachers, and servants like their masters. If the head of the house has been called Beelzebul, how much more the members of his household! [26] "So do not be afraid of them, for there is nothing concealed that will not be disclosed, or hidden that will not be made known. [27] What I tell you in the dark, speak in the daylight; what is whispered in your ear, proclaim from the roofs. [28] **Do not be afraid of those who kill the body but cannot kill the soul.** *Rather, be afraid of the One who can destroy both soul and body in hell. [29] Are not two sparrows sold for a penny? Yet not one of them will fall to the ground outside your Father's care.[30] And*

even the very hairs of your head are all numbered. ³¹ So don't be afraid; you are worth more than many sparrows. ³² "Whoever acknowledges me before others, I will also acknowledge before my Father in heaven. ³³ But whoever disowns me before others, I will disown before my Father in heaven" (Matt. 10:24-33).

Jesus is above us and we are his disciples who aim to become more and more like him. We will share in his glory one day, but in the meantime, we may also share in his persecution. If the persecutors of Jesus would call him Beelzebul, meaning they accused him of working with and being evil (although he was nothing of the kind), and if he is the head, then we will also be persecuted as the members of his household. Jesus said we should not fear persecution despite how our circumstances might seem, because we share in him, which is the most wonderful of things. One day every hidden thing will end up being revealed, including the sins of those who persecute us. We can therefore have great courage as we follow his footsteps, shouting from the rooftops the good news of Jesus.

"Do not be afraid of those who kill the body but cannot kill the soul", this was the verse that was called out by a female member of a group of twelve Elim missionaries as they were being brutally slaughtered at the Elim Mission Station in the Vumba Mountains, in Northern Zimbabwe on Elim's darkest day, 23 June 1978. The thirteenth victim in the same attack died a week later. The sheer brutality of this massacre shocked the world as the story hit both national and international news headlines. Always remember that when we become a disciple of Jesus, we have eternal life and no matter what happens to our bodies, even persecution and death, nothing will separate us from the

love of God. Nothing will fall to the ground in death that is not under the Father's care. If you doubt that care, then please try not to, because he alone has the bigger picture and knows the exact number of hairs on your head. All citizens are of great value to their King.

Will you publicly acknowledge Jesus even when facing some opposition? The bond of love you have with him is even stronger than other relationships that we would naturally stand up for, like protecting our spouse. If we do so, he will one day acknowledge us in return, as he introduces us to our heavenly Father.

Jesus' Mission will divide opinion

"Do not suppose that I have come to bring peace to the earth. I did not come to bring peace, but a sword. ³⁵ For I have come to turn "'a man against his father, a daughter against her mother, a daughter-in-law against her mother-in-law—³⁶ a man's enemies will be the members of his own household"' (Matt. 10:34-36).

Jesus will not automatically bring peace to the earth, even though he is the Prince of Peace. Remember we are here as disciples who carry and distribute his peace, but not all will receive it because humanity still has free will. We see this when we encounter opposition on our journey. Jesus here re-iterates from verse twenty-one, that the Kingdom of Heaven will not mean an absence of hostility, even in our closest relationships. We need therefore to be extra watchful and careful, in order that we might do our best to reach them.

In Conclusion

Although we don't like to suffer, or even to see others suffering, we have to be realistic: it will happen to us all at some point. Relating this to mission, when we go with the message of heaven, we should expect opposition. This can be from our neighbour just down the road, or anywhere on this planet that our feet take us – wherever Jesus sends us.

Therefore, as citizens, we have to stay spiritually alert, so that we can stay in step with the Holy Spirit and be led by him. We are taking the good news of the person probably most hated in history. Never forget that we are to be encouraged by the tremendous and eternal value the Father places upon us and we are not to be afraid, a phrase repeated three times for emphasis (Matt. 10:26, 28, 31). Knowing in advance that the mission of Jesus will divide opinion is both helpful in preparation and comforting in practise. We go despite all these things and we continue acknowledging Jesus before others.

Salvation is free, but discipleship will cost you your life.

CHAPTER EIGHT

Citizens Give Ultimate Loyalty

At the start of Matthew chapter ten Jesus commissions and sends out the twelve disciples on their first-ever mission trip. They are to speak about heaven, they are authorised to demonstrate the Kingdom, they are to give away freely what they have received from Jesus, they must be totally committed, they must carry and distribute the peace of God, and they will face opposition. Under persecution or opposition, it can be much easier to give up, but God has promised to be with us and to speak through us. We know our battle is through prayer (spiritual) and fasting (physical), and that his message will divide even the closest of families as some accept Jesus and others don't. That is the context disciples of Jesus operate in, since that first mission trip. But now Jesus demands an ultimate loyalty above everything else – above anything that could detract or distract the disciples from him as their King.

Matthew writes these next three verses more gently than Luke's parallel does, probably because of his audience being Jewish Christians, who perfectly understand the language of family division around Jesus. The Gentiles, to whom Luke writes, have it put more bluntly. We will review Luke's version later in chapter eleven of this book.

Above Relationships

"Anyone who loves their father or mother more than me is not worthy of me; anyone who loves their son or daughter more than me is not worthy of me" (Matt. 10:37).

We must not have displaced loyalties even to our closest family members or those closest to our hearts. Think for a moment – who is the closest person that you love most? Have you got that someone in your mind? Jesus must come first! If not, we may well refuse to 'take up our cross' and truly follow Jesus; we will lose our life. Correctly prioritising Jesus above these closest of relationships, for the sake and cause of Jesus, enables us to both secure our life and to truly live it.

The phrase *'is not worthy of me'* is repeated a second time in this one short verse. What did Matthew mean exactly, what point was he doubly trying to get across, to help us understand? Well, Jesus is 'worthy', which comes from the word *worth*, or something we value. This is from where we get the old English term worth-ship, which is worship in our modern English. We must worship Jesus. Not being worthy of him does perhaps mean that we will not receive his favour, his benefits and his reward, or even be considered as one of his disciples!

Above Self

"Whoever does not take up their cross and follow me is not worthy of me" (Matt. 10:38).

For a third time, Matthew uses the term *'is not worthy of me'*. Taking up your cross was, and still is, a very serious matter. In the era of the Roman Empire, it meant carrying the tree upon which you were about to be nailed and left to die. Would you be able to suffer a martyr's death like a condemned criminal, for the cause of Jesus and his Kingdom? Could you follow Jesus even if it meant losing your life for him?

Did you know that we are supposed to crucify the flesh with its passions and desires (Gal. 5:24) and that the Bible also tells us that we are to die to self every single day (1 Cor. 15:31)? We must stop thinking in terms of *I think, I feel and I want.* Instead consider what God thinks, what God feels and what God wants. It is in the area of the soul or self (mind, emotions, and will) that we are probably most vulnerable in the moment-by-moment daily opposition that we face. This is where the enemy attacks most. We therefore have to make this choice frequently, to put Jesus and his ways above our own.

Above Possessions

"Whoever finds their life will lose it, and whoever loses their life for my sake will find it" (Matt. 10:39).

'*Whoever finds their life*' refers to those who make their own way, or to put it another way, those who walk the wide path that does not follow closely or depend upon God, having their own control and doing as they please. These are the ones who will lose their lives in the end. The blessings of God will not be there for them, neither will eternal life with God. If the possibility of becoming a martyr or being alienated from family leads us to renounce Jesus or even to deny Jesus his rightful place in our lives, then we will lose our lives.

We secure eternal life, abundant life and a life of freedom now, by losing it! Losing it for the sake of Jesus and his Kingdom message means that we are prepared to forsake all things that we like or want or prefer. We need to see everything we have gained as being because of God's provision, that we are simply stewards of those things and that he remains the owner. All we have should be used to further his Kingdom, and thus we walk the narrow path.

Reward for Mission

"Anyone who welcomes you welcomes me, and anyone who welcomes me welcomes the one who sent me. ⁴¹ Whoever welcomes a prophet as a prophet will receive a prophet's reward, and whoever welcomes a righteous person as a righteous person will receive a righteous person's reward. ⁴² And if anyone gives even a cup of cold water to one of these little ones who is my disciple, truly I tell you, that person will certainly not lose their reward" (Matt. 10:40-42).

After the threat of persecution and alienation in the previous verses, Matthew brings great encouragement as he concludes his tenth chapter.

The context still seems to be those we go to with the message of heaven. The text is about those who welcome or receive Jesus and those who also receive the Father. Even if they welcome and receive a prophet or a righteous man, they will receive these as rewards as well. This reward continues down to even a cup of water. Therefore, anyone who is brand new as a disciple (who may seem less significant than a prophet or righteous man), and is willing to give what they might have to someone else, only giving a cup of water, they too will certainly not lose their reward. The original language does not use the word 'certainly' but it helps to emphasis this as a fact. They will not lose their reward.

Essentially, what we sow we reap (Gal. 6:7). If we generously sow seeds of acceptance of Jesus and his ministry, we will generously reap back these rewards for ourselves (2 Cor. 9:16b) and we will not lose them. If we sow... "*to please the Spirit, from the Spirit will reap eternal life*" (Gal. 6:8b). When we become disciples by choosing to follow Jesus, we become that righteous man as by faith, metaphorically we put on his robes that make us so (Rom. 3:22; 4:24; 6:18; 9:30). From the very beginning, we have more to give away than we might think.

The word prophet is perhaps used here to signify those who speak God's message of the Kingdom, and the word righteous as those who walk an authentic and holy journey of faith, that clearly represents the character of God. Do we walk with the character of God as we proclaim his message, or can we at times be a little hypocritical?

The simplest acts of kindness can be shown by any one of us regardless of our age and ability. You are all included in this mission that Jesus started and left for us to carry on. You can all participate and you are all expected to participate. Think of a war effort. The whole nation would be affected and, in some way, all of its citizens would play a part, no matter how small. The oldest in my church can describe what this was like from the second world war. The ones left at home, who are supporting those out on the front line and in the trenches, are just as vital. All are impacted through separation, isolation, worry and loss; all receive the same reward of victory and a life of freedom. In 2020 and 2021, we have a modern-day example with the Covid-19 pandemic. It is a deadly disease that needed delivery drivers and volunteer staff, as well as the scientists, medical experts and governmental decision makers. These situations both illustrate to us that the mission of Jesus is for every disciple and the whole church community is expected to be actively involved. As the Father sent Jesus as his agent, we too are sent by Jesus to be his agents who speak about the Kingdom of Heaven. What we have freely received we freely pass on. The reward is getting to serve our King and seeing that some will respond positively to him.

Jesus Rules

A true king 'reigns' and he also 'rules' over his Kingdom and his subjects. The wishes of the king are obeyed and they will become law. When a king rules he has no leadership team, no government and no debates. He is not voted in or out, but succeeds through an inherited family line, from the previous king. This might sound more similar to a modern-day peerage in the inherited sense, or even a dictatorship, rather than a democracy in the political sense, as there is no voting or choice in the matter. The Queen of England reigns but she does not rule, this is done through government and in a democratic society that has the vote. Jesus, on the other hand, is King of the Kingdom because his Father is a King, who conferred his Kingdom upon Jesus (Luke 22:29). There was no democratic vote in any of this. Now, that could be very bad if Jesus was a rough King, but Jesus is a very good King, he is the ultimate King.[38]

We often say (and hear other Christians saying) that Jesus reigns, that he is on his throne and in control, which of course is all true. However, Jesus as the King of all kings is now looking for subjects who willingly obey his rules or keep his commands. Christians pray for Jesus to rule in their nation, when in fact Jesus is looking to rule through us as his obedient subjects. This is how we bring the Kingdom of Heaven to planet earth. The trouble is, Jesus cannot find many subjects, because we are all too busy doing what we want and making our own way in life. This helps us to see why in the OT it was not the best choice that Israel made when they asked for their own human king instead of God their divine King. They appointed mere human kings, all of whom were fallible. Their history is now littered with bad kings making bad decisions. God knew all along that he would need to send another divine King to make a way for Israel and the entire human race. When we grasp that Jesus is our divine King, who both reigns and rules, it becomes an honour, privilege and joy to be a subject willing to do what he commands. That is what disciples or citizens of the King do.

In Conclusion

Where exactly are your deepest loyalties as you go out to extend the influence of our Kingdom, amid persecution and opposition? Jesus is looking for ultimate loyalty from you. It is God's great love for us that grants us our freedom both to love

---

[38] Pawson, D. *Kingdoms in Conflict.*

and to loyally serve him.[39] This means being loyal to Jesus above all relationships, above self and above every possession. There is great encouragement in doing so, with the certainty of reward both in this life and for eternity, that will not be lost. By the way, God still allows us to enjoy and love others, our lives and the things he provides for us, but they must mean less to us than he does.

Following our King's rules, including going to others with the message of heaven, is what makes us a true subject, disciple or citizen of the Kingdom.

As we conclude Matthew chapter ten, we can see parallels with the Sermon on the Mount. In our journey we have ventured into chapters eight, nine and ten. Both close with similar challenges: is your house built on the rock or the sand (Matt. 7:24-27) and will you be willing to lose your life to find it (Matt. 10:39). With ultimate loyalty, there can be no middle ground or compromise.

Salvation is free, but discipleship will cost you your life.

---

[39] Boice, J. M. *Foundations of the Christian Faith*, P320.

CHAPTER NINE

Citizens Seek the Father

The next three chapters of Matthew's Gospel, eleven to thirteen, see an increased opposition to the Kingdom of Heaven with sections of unbelief followed by belief. For example, the unbelief of Israel is stressed, then belief in God's sovereignty (Matt. 11:25-30). This example will be our focus, but some events take place before we get there.

Having seen Jesus' demonstration of the Kingdom interwoven with discipleship teaching, we then see him sending out the twelve disciples (Matt. 8-10). As we move into chapter eleven, Jesus heads off on his own to preach in the towns of Galilee – a solo mission. From one of these towns, Jesus ends up speaking to John the Baptist indirectly (who was in prison), and also to John's disciples being his foot messengers who would take the message back to John. Jesus tells them all the things he has been doing to demonstrate the Kingdom. This confirmed Jesus as the one who was to come, the one sent by God (Matt. 11:1-6). As they leave to go back to John, Jesus remains in an unnamed town in the region of Galilee, and speaks to the crowds about John, about the sacrifice John had to make to follow his calling as a prophet. John was the greatest prophet because he carried the greatest message; we as citizens today *carry* the Kingdom within us, and so are greater even than John (Matt. 11:7-11).

It had been since the start of John's ministry that people first began to speak about the King and his coming Kingdom, and opposition against it began to arise... *"the kingdom of heaven has been subjected to violence, and violent people have been raiding it" ["take it by force" ESV and NKJV]* (Matt. 11:12). The difficulty here can be around the original wording, which may be viewed as either negative or positive. By this point in chapter eleven, however, we do have to remember that the overall context was one of increasing persecution.

Jesus has a lot to say about John and even refers to him as the Elijah who was to come. John was divinely appointed to be the forerunner prophet who introduced both the Kingdom itself (Matt. 3:2), and then Jesus, to the world (at Jesus' baptism). Elijah was a unique prophet in that he ascended to heaven like Jesus did (2 Kings 2:11). Elijah had even been held on par with the great Moses. In the final book of the OT, Elijah is again mentioned... *"See, I will send the prophet Elijah to you before that great and dreadful day of the Lord comes"* (Mal. 4:5). Only those with spiritual insight would see and recognise that John the Baptist held this incredible Elijah-like ministry that the Malachi scripture foretold. The point for us today is that it doesn't matter what we are called, or falsely accused of, for following Jesus into his mission. In the end, the wisdom of the message we proclaim will be proved right (Matt. 11:12-19).

Jesus then denounces three Galilean towns named Chorazin, Bethsaida and Capernaum – whose people did not repent as John had warned them to, after the amazing miracles that they had witnessed (Matt. 11:20-24).

And what of Jesus' disciples? I wonder how they were getting on with their mission trip? There were no mobile phones, texting, or video messaging technology; the verses here don't update us. However, it is at the end of this outpouring from Jesus' heart, where he expresses great rejection of himself and his mission, that we come to the most incredible prayer.

The Father Revealed in the Son and by the Son

"At that time Jesus said, 'I praise you, Father, Lord of heaven and earth, because you have hidden these things from the wise and learned, and revealed them to little children. ²⁶ Yes, Father, for this is what you were pleased to do. ²⁷ 'All things have been committed to me by my Father. No one knows the Son except the Father, and no one knows the Father except the Son and those to whom the Son chooses to reveal him. ²⁸ 'Come to me, all you who are weary and burdened, and I will give you rest. ²⁹ Take my yoke upon you and learn from me, for I am gentle and humble in heart, and you will find rest for your souls. ³⁰ For my yoke is easy and my burden is light'" (Matt. 11:25-30).

Jesus' prayer had been recorded and therefore Jesus must have spoken it aloud to people. We cannot be sure he has moved on anywhere else, the text simply says 'at that time', and he is most likely still in an unnamed town in Galilee, talking to the same people. Perhaps John's disciples were still in ear-shot too. Either way, Jesus wanted his prayer to be heard. This section records the innermost thoughts and prayers of Jesus' heart. If you want to really get to know someone, then pray regularly with them and you will soon be able to tell what is in their heart... *"For the mouth speaks what the heart is full of"* (Matt. 12:34; Luke 6:45).

Do you collapse in a heap when opposition comes? What about when that opposition grows and intensifies? Jesus is experiencing increasing opposition and has just poured out his inmost feelings and frustrations. We should learn how Jesus handles this and apply his way of dealing with it into our lives. What does he do? He turns toward, and gets his strength and comfort from his Father. It is so simple, but we often seem to forget to do this ourselves, or am I the only one?

Jesus starts with **praise and position**. The Father is always worthy of praise no matter what happens, however hard things might be and whether your situation is fair or not. Then Jesus states out loud who his Father truly is, and the position he holds over everything, over heaven and earth. Resetting the true context of our heavenly Father within us helps us recalibrate and see whatever our opposition happens to be, in a much better context. We can be very good at 'making mountains out of mole-hills'; remembering who our heavenly Father is will reverse that.

Jesus recalls that the Father has hidden the things of the Kingdom from wise people and revealed it to those with child-like attitudes of trust, love, obedience and hope. The Father in his sovereignty hid some things from the wise and showed them to those who might seem insignificant. So, if you ever feel insignificant like a child might, then you are in good company because the Father will reveal spiritual truths to you. A child also recognises its dependence upon its parents, which is true for us as children of the Father. Acknowledging this aloud helps to completely ease Jesus' frustrations as well as bringing comfort in his rejection. Wouldn't that be great if we too could have our frustrations and feelings of rejection sorted? Well, now you at least know where to start (Matt. 11:25).

To know the heart of Jesus we can look at his prayers. In this one, we must note that **whatever pleased the Father was of most concern to Jesus**. He reminds himself that it is the Father who has committed everything to him. He remembers his purpose, the greater cause of his mission and why he has been sent. Then increasing opposition can 'sit back down' in its rightful place within. Who are you praying with regularly that knows your heart? It is always good to pray with others to help you in staying on track with your heart responses. Is pleasing the Father also your greatest concern? If not, then I believe it should be. We all wanted at some point to please our earthly parents and have their approval. How much more should we seek to please our heavenly Father? Doing this will make your discipleship journey run much more smoothly. The external circumstances may not change, but internal turmoil will get recalibrated. If that has been a difficulty in your life, please try learning to do what Jesus did (Matt. 11:26).

The Father has committed all things to Jesus, which means that the Father completely trusts the Son, and the Son knows this to be true. Sounds easy enough, but did you ever try and teach your children to drive? I was a nervous wreck, panicking at every turn because I could not jump in and help; we didn't have a dual control car. As their father, I'm pretty sure they were fully aware that my presence was not a helpful one – more like a dreadful one. That was nothing to do with their driving by the way as they are both very good, but I was not able to completely trust what their inexperience might do. This is not the case with Father and Son, who have total trust in one another. Amazingly they both also place this level of trust in us, to extend the influence of his Kingdom, despite our lack of experience.

The prayer continues, stating that no person truly knows the Father except Jesus and vice versa. This is because they are made from the same DNA if you like, or perhaps better put, they are of the same essence. The disciples did know the Son, just not as intimately as the Father did, so this is not a literal statement. However, humanity will never be able to grasp the fullness of God, Father, Son or Holy Spirit, this side of eternity. And yet now come the most incredible words... "*no one knows the Father except the Son **and those to whom the Son chooses to reveal him**"*. This means that the Father is knowable to those that Jesus decides to reveal the Father to. I believe that Jesus will and does still reveal the Father to those who are seeking to know the Father. We also know from other scriptures that we have access to the Father... "*For through him [Jesus] we both have access to the Father by one Spirit*" (Eph. 2:18), just not as intimately as the Son does. Have you ever asked Jesus to reveal the Father to you? If you haven't then perhaps that could be a new way to approach your prayers – by desiring to walk in step with the Spirit, to be transformed into the likeness of the Son and to seek the Father and do his will. Hey, does that sound familiar? That was essentially the definition of a disciple that was offered earlier in this book.

In my own life, when I sought God over a prolonged period, with all my heart, the Father was revealed to me by way of a heavenly visitation, perhaps similar to Paul (2 Cor. 12:1-6), so

I know that this is a possibility for each one of us. Are you desperate for an encounter with him? **Disciples will seek to know their heavenly Father**. The Father and Son reside in heaven at this time and it is God the Holy Spirit who forms the character of Jesus within us, and the same Holy Spirit who can show us the Father (Matt. 11:27).

We are invited to go to Jesus and accept the rest he offers. *Rest* might be more accurately translated as *relief*. Whether it is rest or relief from the opposition you are facing, it is only because of the intimate relationship and knowledge of his Father, that Jesus offers us to come to him, knowing he is able to give this to us. His promise of rest happens to also come right before chapter twelve in Matthew, which looks at the Sabbath rest.

Jesus doesn't burden us with religious baggage that will weigh us down. Instead, he offers us to learn from his approach, and because he is gentle and humble we can inherit this promise of rest as children of the same Father. Whilst others will oppress and persecute us, Jesus won't. We can allow circumstances to get the better of us can't we, and then it feels hard or impossible to even follow Jesus. Yet, while our challenge when following him on mission can be dire, if we do follow his example in approaching our heavenly Father, things will take their rightful perspective, a Kingdom perspective that will still enable us to walk with joy (Matt. 11:28-30).

In Conclusion

When we as citizens of the Kingdom face growing opposition through physical or spiritual challenges, we must learn to do what Jesus did. We go back to the basics of praising and correctly re-positioning the Father in our hearts and minds to his true and rightful position. The things we face just won't seem so difficult when we do that.

Aiming to please our Father, through obedience and trusting what he says, must be a disciple's first concern. We are to have the same heart as Jesus in seeking the Father – that Jesus made possible to access. Why would we ever not want to seek our heavenly Father?

Jesus still reveals the Father today, to those who in their weariness choose to rest in all that Jesus is, and who are childlike, gentle, humble, innocent and pure... *"Blessed are the pure in heart, for they will see God"* (Matt. 5:8). Are you seeking the Father with every fibre of your being, with a desperation to encounter him?

Salvation is free, but discipleship will cost you your life.

CHAPTER TEN

Citizens Take Up Their Cross

I want to highlight some of the journey and context of what is happening in the build-up to one of Jesus' strongest statements about what it means, in his view, to be one of his disciples; to take up your own cross, in Matthew chapter sixteen.

In chapter twelve Jesus continues to demonstrate the Kingdom by declaring that he is Lord of even the Sabbath, that one greater than Jonah and one greater than Solomon is right in front of them... *"Pointing to his disciples, he said, "Here are my mother and my brothers. For whoever does the will of my Father in heaven is my brother and sister and mother""* (Matt. 12:49-50). This neatly sums up the previous chapter in this book.

Chapter thirteen of Matthew then contains seven parables that describe what the Kingdom of heaven is like. These are covered in some detail in the first book in this Kingdom Perspective series: *Territory of the Kingdom*.

Chapter fourteen shows that disciples should expect to be a part of the solution, like in feeding the five-thousand Jewish people. We should remain expectant of both seeing and doing strange things, like Jesus walking on the water and then Peter joining him. Disciples are a people of faith, no matter how ridiculous they might seem to others today. If we saw what looked like a ghost of Jesus walking on water, how on earth would we respond? Run away probably, but no, we should be willing to go out to him on the water ourselves. Whilst we may never actually do that particular feat, our expectation should certainly be for the impossible, because that is what he is the God of. This is therefore likely to remain metaphorical for us, but are we people of real faith? Other examples today might be when the Holy Spirit manifests in power and people are then physically overcome, or when hearing the screams of demons when they are cast out. Is that all too much for our nice, neat and tidy faith? These things should not scare or confuse us, rather we should roll up our sleeves and join the praying army to help minister to people and set them free.

Chapter fifteen shows that we need to be willing to give the little we have for the purposes of God, like in feeding the four thousand Gentiles, or foreigners.

In reaching chapter sixteen we see the need for disciples to desire and seek heavenly wisdom and revelation from the Father... *"this was not revealed to you by flesh and blood, but by my Father in heaven"* (Matt. 16:17). If we do, then Jesus will give us the keys of his Kingdom of Heaven. Jesus entrusts the possession of its key – prayer – to each of us as his stewards.

Jesus' Suffering

"From that time on Jesus began to explain to his disciples that he must go to Jerusalem and suffer many things at the hands of the elders, the chief priests and the teachers of the law, and that he must be killed and on the third day be raised to life. Peter took him aside and began to rebuke him. 'Never, Lord!' he said. 'This shall never happen to you!'" (Matt. 16:21-22).

Jesus speaks for the first time about his predicted passion, that he must go to the cross, suffer an agonising death at the hands of a united Israeli leadership and be raised again to life. The chief priests were Sadducees, the teachers of the law were Scribes who taught the Pharisees, and together with the elders they all made up the Supreme Court, known as the Sanhedrin. United they condemned him. Jesus teaches this to the disciples four times: here in 16:21 and also in 17:22-23; 20:17-19 and 26:1-2. We must also expect and be willing to suffer for our faith. Jesus would willingly go to the cross and that challenge is about to become ours.

Peter misunderstands God's plan for the Messiah and contests this prediction. Jesus' reply could hardly have been sterner… "*Get behind me Satan. You are a stumbling-block to me; you do not have in mind the concerns of God, but merely human concerns*" (Matt. 16:23). This is the complete opposite of Peter earlier receiving divine revelation about the Messiah. Just a few moments later Peter walks in the natural realm, out of step with the Spirit, and messes it up! How often do we do that: walk in the Spirit and then walk in the flesh? **We must not get in the way of the Father's will but rather align ourselves with it**. Perhaps Peter only heard that Jesus would be killed and the words about the resurrection did not properly register. We can be like Peter too and focus on our current and immediate troubles instead of our eternal glory.

Jesus' Model of Discipleship

Jesus now uses this teaching opportunity to clearly explain to his disciples what it means to truly follow him. The very next thing he says is… "*Whoever wants to be my disciple must deny*

themselves and take up their cross and follow me. ²⁵ For whoever
wants to save their life will lose it, but whoever loses their life for
me will find it. ²⁶ What good will it be for someone to gain the
whole world, yet forfeit their soul? Or what can anyone give in
exchange for their soul? ²⁷ For the Son of Man is going to come
in his Father's glory with his angels, and then he will reward each
person according to what they have done. ²⁸ 'Truly I tell you,
some who are standing here will not taste death before they see
the Son of Man coming in his kingdom.' (Matt. 16:24-28).

Citizens of the Kingdom must do these three things... 1) deny
themselves, 2) take up their cross, and 3) follow Jesus. This is
the essence of discipleship as Jesus sees it. Jesus never wastes
an opportunity to help someone grow in their understanding
and ability to follow him. Off the back of that sharp rebuke of
Peter, he seizes this moment to drive home the importance of
the cross – the centrality of the cross to all disciples. The cross
comes before the crown, the suffering before the glory. If this
was the case for Jesus it will be the case for us too.

Deny yourself means the death of self. If you picked up a cross
you would be walking it to your own execution. When you face
death, suddenly all of your priorities change and what is most
important comes rushing to the fore. For us, as disciples living
today, it means dying to me – my desires, my wants, my
pleasures, my attitudes, my wealth, my thinking, my feelings
and living instead for him. Paul puts it like this... *"For you died,*
and your life is now hidden with Christ in God" (Col. 3:3), and...
"Here is a trustworthy saying: If we died with him, we will also
live with him" (2 Tim. 2:11), and... *"he died for all, that those*

who live should no longer live for themselves but for him who died for them and was raised again" (2 Cor. 5:15).

Having chosen to deny yourself, next comes the choice to **take up your cross.** Luke adds the word 'daily' to Matthew's account (Luke 9:23), meaning it is an everyday choice for the rest of our lives (we die to ourselves and instead live for Christ). Carrying a cross was both hard work and a visible sign of submission. Does your life outwardly display continual loving submission and obedience to Jesus, following all of his commands as someone continuing his mission (Matt. 16:24)?

To **follow Jesus** requires going the route that he laid out for us. I recall a time when my daughter Sasha was about six years of age, and was leading our group walking along a narrow bendy pathway through some crop fields. The crops on either side were taller than she was and we could only fit in single file; I was right behind her. My shoelace came undone and so I naturally stopped for a few moments to retie it, holding up the rest of the group. Unawares, Sasha continued walking and we quickly lost sight of her as she rounded the next bend. Having tied the lace, I jumped up and ran to catch up with her and all was well. Some lessons from this story: 1) as I caught up with Sasha, God spoke to me and said "never lead too far ahead of your people". This was helpful advice that I have always tried to adhere to in leadership so that people do not lose sight of our God-given direction and vision, 2) although the pathway may be narrow, we can be clearly guided where to go even if we become detached from our leader through the twists and turn of life. God is able to keep us on the right track, and 3) it is very easy to quickly become out of step with the Holy Spirit as well as with our leaders; we need to catch up as quickly as we can and stay working in unity together.

Following Jesus will require staying close to him, on the path and direction he has for your life and the life of your church or ministry, and remaining in unity whether you are pushing along at the front or doing your best at keeping up. I have mentioned earlier, that to follow is not only a route that we take, but is to become like Jesus in every way.

Self-preservation in this life will often lead to self-destructive decisions and choices, whereas, self-denial to benefit others will often lead to self-fulfilment, because we know that it is better for us when we give rather than receive (Acts 20:35). You cannot save yourself and you cannot avoid the cross. Try and bypass the work of Jesus in and through you and you will lose your life. Accept the cross and Jesus' ways, and you will find your Saviour and your Lord; you will find life. That is what Jesus came to give us: a life that is worth living now despite its troubles, and on into eternity with God. Perhaps think about the 'Lord of the Manor'. Our Lord is the owner and ruler of all that goes on in his territory. Your territory is your body and your inner life, but who is in charge? Is it you, or have you let Jesus truly be your Lord (Matt. 16:25)?

You can gain as much money, property, cars and material things you like, but they will make no difference to whether your soul will end up in heaven or hell. Jesus is telling you to sort out your destiny and your life on this planet first, to seek first the Kingdom (Matt. 6:33). If you do gain material things as well that is ok, but if you don't, there should be no need to complain. Paul learnt to be content in all situations he faced, whether in plenty or in lack (Phil. 4:11-12). The writer to the Hebrew believers puts it this way... *"Keep your lives free from the love of money and be content with what you have, because God has said, "Never will I leave you; never will I forsake you.""* (Heb. 13:5). You cannot buy your salvation and your eternity in heaven, no matter how much money you might have. Being content is important and knowing Jesus will never leave you should aid you in that contentment. Perhaps this is exactly what hymn writer Horatio Spafford had discovered, in the middle of life's most difficult personal circumstances. Are you able to join his song, is it well with your soul? (Matt. 16:26).

We do need reminding regularly of Kingdom values and that both his glory and our reward await us as disciples. It is better to focus on those things than on our present troubles, because then we are able to live a life of self-denial and service both for Jesus and with Jesus, regardless of the cost, even if that means making the ultimate sacrifice. The more that we are able do in spreading the influence of this spiritual Kingdom, the greater our reward will be. I believe that reward will be in this present life, not with material riches but fullness of life, both now, and onwards into eternity (Matt. 16:27).

Jesus said that some of his very first disciples, who were there with him, would not die before they will get to see Jesus in his Kingdom. This probably refers to Jesus' resurrection, his coming back from death, not his future return for the Church known as his second coming. It could also potentially refer to his transfiguration (which appears in the very next chapter of Matthew), his ascension back into heaven, or perhaps the day of Pentecost. But mostly like he is referring to his resurrection. Can you imagine being there and witnessing first hand Jesus' transfiguration, resurrection, ascension and the outpouring of the Spirit of Jesus? Glorious indeed (Matt. 16:28)!

In Conclusion

If you want to be a disciple of Jesus you absolutely must do these three things: die to yourself, take up your cross and follow him. Jesus offers no caveats here, no separate clause for trying and difficult circumstances, no excuses, even if it ends up costing you everything. Jesus suffered in his ministry and we as his citizens continuing that same ministry, will no doubt also suffer at times. We have been pre-warned and such situations should not take us by surprise and throw us off course, as we journey along his narrow path for our lives. This means being content in all that we face. If we think about the glories of Jesus that the first disciples got to witness, we will not be left out. We know that he will never leave or forsake us, that we will see his glory one day and we will be rewarded for our service.

Does Jesus mean so much to you that, as he promises you, you will also never leave him? A life of total surrender, everything you are and everything you have, now belong to your King. Your life is not your own, it was bought with a price... "*Do you not know that your bodies are temples of the Holy Spirit, who is in you, whom you have received from God? You are not your own; 20 you were bought at a price*" (1 Cor. 6:19-20a). We are called to die to ourselves and to live for Christ.

Salvation is free, discipleship will cost you your life!

CHAPTER ELEVEN

Citizenship Essentials

Now we will divert away from Matthew, venturing into Luke's Gospel, and explore his similar but slightly different reasons on what a disciple is and isn't. In Luke chapter nine, he adds the important word 'daily', meaning that for the rest of our lives on this earth, we are to deny ourselves take up our cross and follow Jesus. Then in chapter fourteen, we see Luke using much stronger language than Matthew does: with words like "hate", and "cannot be my disciple". In shocking paradox, Jesus gives reasons why and how a person cannot be a disciple.[40] Therefore, we need to take a closer look into this rather strong terminology that Luke is presenting to a predominately Greek initial audience, to see what other foundational elements must also be embedded into our journeying with Jesus.

"Large crowds were travelling with Jesus, and turning to them he said:[26] **"If anyone comes to me and does not hate father and mother, wife and children, brothers and sisters—yes, even their own life—such a person cannot be my disciple.** *[27]* **And whoever does not carry their cross and follow me cannot be my disciple.** *[28]* *"Suppose one of you wants to build a tower. Won't you first sit down and estimate the cost to see if you have enough money to complete it?[29] For if you lay the foundation and*

---

[40] Willard, D. *Renovation of the Heart. Putting on the Character of Christ* (Nottingham: Inter-Varsity Press, 2002), P51.

are not able to finish it, everyone who sees it will ridicule you, ³⁰
saying, 'This person began to build and wasn't able to finish.' ³¹
"Or suppose a king is about to go to war against another king.
Won't he first sit down and consider whether he is able with ten
thousand men to oppose the one coming against him with twenty
thousand? ³² *If he is not able, he will send a delegation while the*
other is still a long way off and will ask for terms of peace. ³³ *In*
the same way, **those of you who do not give up everything you**
have cannot be my disciples. ³⁴ *"Salt is good, but if it loses its*
saltiness, how can it be made salty again? ³⁵ *It is fit neither for*
the soil nor for the manure pile; it is thrown out. "Whoever has
ears to hear, let them hear"" (Luke 14:25-35).

The Crowds

In this text, we see that large crowds were travelling with and
following Jesus. Jesus was likely heading towards Jerusalem
and people were expecting him to overthrow the Roman
authorities there and set up his own earthly kingdom.[41] How
wrong they were... *"My kingdom is not of this world"* (John
18:36)!

When Jesus sees the crowd around him and people wanting to
follow him, he becomes a little sceptical of their true loyalty.
He 'lays it out there' or puts it in simple words using quite blunt
language, essentially to check that people are completely sure
that they do want to follow him. Barclay uses the helpful
example of someone that attends a lecture who may not be a

---

[41] Barclay, W. *The Gospel of Luke* (Edinburgh: The Saint Andrew Press,
1960), P203.

real student – attending a lecture and actually learning can be very different things – a world apart.[42]

Today, we often want to find people that will become followers of us don't we. How many followers do you have on Instagram? has become an important question in our social media world. We want to draw a crowd and then to keep them and to please them, so that they keep on following us and supporting us. This gives us personal acclaim, good standing with people and even a way of making money.

Jesus had said earlier that... *"foxes have dens and birds have nests, but the Son of Man has no place to lay his head"* (Luke 9:58). In other words, I have nowhere to sleep tonight, so are you sure you want to follow me? Jesus continues here in this style of rhetoric, to clearly state what it truly means to be his disciple.

Jesus turns to these enthusiastic followers in order to lay down the terms of what it really means to follow him. He gave three conditions that need to be met to be his disciple: 1) hate your loved ones, 2) give up your own life, and 3) give up all of your possessions (Luke 14:25).

Hate Your Loved Ones – Cannot Number One

Luke's text does appear to contradict other scriptures, for example... *"Whoever claims to love God yet hates a brother or sister is a liar. For whoever does not love their brother and sister, whom they have seen, cannot love God, whom they have not*

---

[42] Barclay, W. *The Gospel of Luke*, P203.

seen" (1 John 4:20), and to... "*Honour your father and your mother*" (Exod. 20:12). What is it that Jesus is trying to get across?

As Luke attributes these words to Jesus, his intended audience would have been unlikely to know the OT; for them, there would therefore not have been any contradiction. For us today, who do know of them, there might appear to be some, so we have to dig a little deeper to grasp the meaning.

It is not that you literally have to hate your loved ones, as that would make no sense. The Greek word hate, *miseó*, means to love someone or something less. Therefore, whenever there might be a conflict of loyalty Jesus must take priority. Our love for Jesus should be so great that others are loved less. Like our faith, discipleship involves both a starting point and a journey, entry and continuation. In the continuation, if Jesus isn't our first love, then we will struggle with always being divided and pulled in other directions.[43] He is a treasure so great and so far above everyone that if we see and understand this, then everything else will be worth less than him in our eyes and in our actions. However, doing this could produce difficulties in our families or in our relationships, and will be hard for others not following Jesus to comprehend; but there is no alternative that Jesus provides.

When Peter and the apostles were being questioned by the court, they replied... "*we must obey God rather than human*

---

[43] Bock, D. L. *Luke Vol. 2: 9:51-24:53* (Grand Rapids: Baker Academic, 1996), P1284-5.

beings" (Acts 5:29), demonstrating that their greatest love and loyalty, lay rightly with Jesus (Luke 14:26).

Give Up Your Life – Cannot Number Two

As Jesus moves towards having to take up his own cross and give up his own life as a ransom for many, he is checking if the crowds are still sure that they want to follow him. It cannot get much more critical than giving up your life. Who in their right mind, would want to follow someone travelling along that path? However, Jesus is saying that if you are not willing to pick up your cross and walk with me and essentially die on a cross next to me, if it's not "all in", then no need to bother. A man or woman walking to their execution would have no further plans of their own, they have forfeited control of both their life and their destiny.

Jesus paints this picture so vividly because it was going to be his reality and a reality for some of his first disciples. Even today, some disciples are faced with denouncing Jesus through torture and an actual threat of losing their lives. But this is not the literal case for the majority of his disciples. Jesus must therefore have been meaning literally for some and giving a stark warning to the rest, that unless you are fully prepared to die for the King and his Kingdom, then you cannot be a disciple. We all must lovingly surrender control of our self, our life and our destiny, to the one who truly loves us. Isn't that what authentic relationship is?

Using the image of death portrays the meaning that if these foundational basics are not followed, then other teachings of

Jesus cannot be learnt and a follower cannot progress into, or succeed as, a disciple (Luke 14:27).[44]

Two Parables

Jesus then uses two parables to illustrate assessing the cost of discipleship,[45] because he wants us to know exactly what we are letting ourselves in for. A disciple must be prepared to pay any price to love and obey Jesus by applying his teachings in their daily living.

In the first parable, a builder has a free choice but needs to work out if he can afford to follow Jesus,[46] because a building only half-built is a mockery. We cannot follow Jesus half-heartedly or we will be exposed as a hypocrite. The world out there, if they know we are Christian, can spot a mile off if our actions do not match up to our faith. If they can, then I think Jesus can too. Bock puts it this way... *"The uncommitted disciple is like a builder who cannot complete a planned project or a foolish king who enters a war he cannot win"*.[47]

In the second parable a king under siege is forced to act and needs to work out if he can refuse Jesus demands.[48] Jesus calls us to a war, a spiritual battle. So think about what you are about to enter into, count the cost first and then sign up, because the

---

[44] Willard, D. *Renovation of the Heart*, P51.

[45] Bock, D. L. *Luke Vol. 2: 9:51-24:53*, P1282.

[46] Morris, L. *Luke. An Introduction and Commentary. Tyndale New Testament Commentaries* (Leicester: Inter-Varsity Press, 1980), P236.

[47] Bock, D. L. *Luke Vol. 2: 9:51-24:53*, P1292.

[48] Morris, L. *Luke. An Introduction and Commentary*, P236.

price could be extremely high. No country or king enters into war lightly, but they think hard about it first and weigh up all of their options. Knowing the cost, but loving the cause even more, is what makes us willing to fight and pay any price. Jesus has already won the victory for us, both long term (eternity) and short term (our life here in preparation for eternity); whilst we may suffer, we cannot lose.

Do we today, make it too easy to follow Jesus? by just getting someone to pray the prayer of salvation, so that we can chalk up one more heaven-bound person. We do absolutely want people to accept Jesus, no question, but we are supposed to make disciples of them. I wonder sometimes if we give people a free entrance pass without explaining what it will cost them.

You do need to know that it's going to be hard at some point, or even at many points, to follow Jesus. We have to know and understand the cost expected of us, so that we will recognise these as 'touch points' only and not simply give up. Jesus did not promise us a mansion on this earth (in heaven, yes, but here, no), he does however say that you might have nowhere to sleep if you follow him. So, figure out the cost of discipleship before you call yourself a disciple. Don't start and not be able to finish. That is what a fool does. Strong stuff, isn't it?

Discipleship is demanding, so one must assess the risk and then, despite knowing those risks, move on confidently with the assigned tasks, thereby remaining useful in extending the influence of the Kingdom (Luke 14:28-32).[49]

---

49 Bock, D. L. *Luke Vol. 2: 9:51-24:53*, P1292.

Give Up All Possessions – Cannot Number Three

We have a lot to renounce or give up because of the fact that we have a lot of stuff, particularly in the first world. If we have nothing, like many in the third world, then perhaps this might be easier to do. But even if we have only one thing in this world, it is still possible to hold onto that one thing too dearly and not be willing to renounce or give it up.

For Jesus it was not about the crowds per se or the size of his following, it's all about discipleship and those who will truly follow him, go for him, and proclaim him to others. Jesus is really clear: he gave everything for us, gives everything to us and he expects everything back from us... *"Jesus answered, "If you want to be perfect, go, sell your possessions and give to the poor, and you will have treasure in heaven. Then come, follow me." When the young man heard this, he went away sad, because he had great wealth"* (Matt. 19:21-22).

I'm fortunate enough to own a Taylor guitar. When I first purchased it, I also bought the t-shirt, the mug and a few other branded items too. God soon challenged me because I had become proud. I simply felt prompted that I should give away the smaller items, which I did. I kept the original blessing of the guitar. I later had a second guitar of the same brand, that I did give away. We come into this world with nothing and we will take nothing with us. Why do we get so obsessed with things? We should distance ourselves from too great an attachment to material things, because they can be destructive for our discipleship journey making us less productive.[50]

Not my will, but yours be done, was how Jesus prayed in the garden of Gethsemane as he faced the anguish of an impending trial, execution, temporary separation from his Father and the weight of this world's sin. We often pray this same pray too. It is a demonstration of the deepest love when someone places the needs of others before their own. How might that apply to us today? Not my house Lord, but how can I use it to bless others? Not my money Lord, but how should I give? Following Jesus does not mean that we have to give everything away and literally have nothing, although it could for some. It does mean that nothing should have such a hold on us, or such a place in our hearts, that we cannot give it up should he ask that of us (Luke 14:33).

Useless Salt

The three *cannot* statements are not about entry requirements into the Kingdom; instead they are to show us that authentic, real discipleship must embrace each one. These commitments must be fully encapsulated into daily living so that we can grow in them. Otherwise, we will be stunted in our growth.[51] Some disciples do not produce as they should, even becoming useless, because they have not dealt with the three *cannot* distractions.[52]

---

[50] Bock, D. L. *Luke Vol. 2: 9:51-24:53*, P1290.

[51] Ibid, P1280.

[52] Ibid, P1292.

If we don't learn to follow Jesus in these ways, then we will not grow into mature disciples. We will remain sat in our comfort zone and lose our saltiness, which will make us virtually useless to the King and his Kingdom. We know that salt preserves, flavours and helps things to flourish, which is exactly what we are supposed to do as well. Jesus did not come to planet earth to live a comfy life, to be waited on hand and foot like a king. No, he came to make a difference, the ultimate difference, which cost him the ultimate price.

Have you ever felt in your heart, or possibly even heard others say, these kinds of things in your church: 'not that song again', 'someone's sitting in my seat', or even, 'there are no chocolate biscuits this week'. Petty things in comparison aren't they, but we do think them. So why exactly do you go to church and what part do you play? Whilst our gathering together is about us being blessed, we should come wishing more to be a blessing to others. How can I help someone today and who might I be able to encourage?

If our character becomes diluted by self-desire and is overly influenced by the world, we will lose our effectiveness both inside the church and outside in the community. Disciples are supposed to be salt and light – useful to and illuminating Jesus. He cannot use us if we lose our saltiness (Luke 14:34-35).

In Conclusion

It is possible to be a follower or inquirer of Jesus but not a true disciple, someone just hanging in the crowds. This will impact our personal life, the lives of those around us, the life of our church and any wider ministries we are involved in. Barclay put it this way... "*It is one of the supreme handicaps of the church that in it there are so many distant followers of Jesus and so few real disciples*".[53] Jesus is turning the spotlight on us; he is stark, blunt and very clear about what will eliminate effective discipleship. The words "cannot be my disciple" condemn any half-heartedness and warn against just being an interested follower.[54] Jesus wants both full-blooded and whole-hearted disciples that place him first, above relationships, above self and above possessions. Doing so will remove the barriers that prevent our growth. We might appear to be losing everything but we gain a priceless relationship and the most incredible life of adventure, lived 'out of the boat' as it were, whilst remaining effective.

It can at times be difficult to be a disciple, but certainly not impossible. The Father's plan was to send his Son to rescue us, the Holy Spirit to partner with us, and to provide heavens resources that enable us to make it as disciples. We now have to play our part and no-one or no-thing, not even ourselves, should be loved and treasured more than Jesus. He who has ears...are you hearing this?

Salvation is free, discipleship will cost you your life!

---

[53] Barclay, W. *The Gospel of Luke*, P203.
[54] Morris, L. *Luke. An Introduction and Commentary*, P237.

CHAPTER TWELVE

Additional Costs of Citizenship

In this final chapter, I want to briefly tease out some additional costs or requirements for every disciple, with a quick glance across the rest of Matthew.

Have Faith

"Then the disciples came to Jesus in private and asked, 'Why couldn't we drive it out?' [20] *He replied, 'Because you have so little faith. Truly I tell you, if you have faith as small as a mustard seed, you can say to this mountain, "Move from here to there," and it will move. Nothing will be impossible for you"'* (Matt. 17:19-20).

Citizens know their King, and if we additionally understand the true magnificence of the Kingdom that Jesus confers on us, then we have every basis needed to be a people of amazing faith. Only faith-filled people are able to do the works that Jesus did. The potential cost for us is that we could look stupid or do things that make us feel embarrassed. Noah is a great example, building an ark, miles away from any water. Everyone mocked him. He continued in faith and obedience and was proved right in the end. God did not let him down. What about today and say, for example, the faith to drive out a demon? Could that upset our nice cosy gatherings? Would we feel embarrassed by the noise, and what some might think?

Jesus usually went about amazing others. Only twice is Jesus himself amazed. One was positive amazement, seeing the faith of the Roman centurion for Jesus to be able to heal by his word and from a distance i.e. without his usual physical touch (Matt. 8:5-10). The other was negative amazement, for the complete lack of faith of the Jews in his home town of Nazareth (Matt. 13:53-58). Our ministry for Jesus must be based upon faith, otherwise, we won't be able to please him (Heb. 11:6). Faith is not a feeling it is an action, but it is also a spiritual gift that God frequently gives us a supernatural amount of. The seemingly impossible situations that we face will then be overcome and everything that is godly will become possible.

Be Good Stewards

"'What do you think, Simon?' he [Jesus] asked. 'From whom do the kings of the earth collect duty and taxes – from their own children or from others?' [26] 'From others,' Peter answered. 'Then the children are exempt,' Jesus said to him. [27] 'But so that we may not cause offence, go to the lake and throw out your line. Take the first fish you catch; open its mouth and you will find a four-drachma coin. Take it and give it to them for my tax and yours'" (Matt. 17:25-27).

Disciples must be good stewards of their finances, paying bills and taxes on time, or we will cause offence, not forgetting of course, to allow for God to provide for us (miracles allowed). And when he does provide, all of it is his and we must be willing to give it up or use it for his Kingdom, for the poor and for our local church. Jesus anticipates their question and starts up the discussion. Good stewardship is always well prepared, thinking ahead and ensuring the right decisions are made. The potential cost here is one of sacrificial and generous giving, done from a joyous heart, not only to pay our bills but also to bless others. Sometimes it will seem to be costly to do the right thing, but in the long run and for inner peace, the benefits will far outweigh the cost.

Be Humble

"*At that time the disciples came to Jesus and asked, 'Who, then, is the greatest in the kingdom of heaven?' [2] He called a little child to him, and placed the child among them. [3] And he said: 'Truly I tell you, unless you change and become like little children, you will never enter the kingdom of heaven. [4] Therefore, whoever takes the lowly position of this child is the greatest in the kingdom of heaven. [5] And whoever welcomes one such child in my name welcomes me*" (Matt. 18:1-5 also see Matt. 19:13-15).

Disciples must become like a child, imitating their own natural dependence upon God, displaying and honouring others with a childlike spirit. Lowly means being humble and that is a constant choice. It does not mean that we are walked over by everyone else, but that we know our position of privilege in the Kingdom and as we grow in knowing our King, we recognise that is what he is. The cost is to put others first. Jesus did this and you can read all about how he did (see Phil. 2): the King became lowly and in human form to embrace our world and to die for its sin.

Be Serving

"*Jesus called them together and said, 'You know that the rulers of the Gentiles lord it over them, and their high officials exercise authority over them. [26] Not so with you. Instead, whoever wants to become great among you must be your servant, [27] and whoever wants to be first must be your slave – [28] just as the Son of Man did not come to be served, but to serve, and to give his life as a ransom for many"* (Matt. 20:25-28).

In referring to the Roman occupation and government over Israel, Jesus teaches a lesson on servanthood. The Jews did not like foreign powers ruling in authority over them. We too are often not pleased when the political party we voted for is not in power. Nonetheless, a servant will always serve those in authority over them with right heart motives, no matter how long the time period. This type of serving is a key principle in Kingdom life. Self-promotion to gain power is the opposite of what disciples should do. Rather, disciples should be practising the laws of the Kingdom. The cost is that we remain and serve well. If Jesus our King served, then surely we too must serve.

Pray and Intercede

"If you believe, you will receive whatever you ask for in prayer" (Matt. 21:22).

I would say that disciples of Jesus are those who believe, although that belief can often waver. It is not always easy to believe especially, when things aren't going according to plan. Belief and faith are things that accompany the life of every disciple. We cannot do without them, just like food and water. They are expressed physically in action and spiritually in prayer and moving in the gifts of the Spirit. Prayer and faith must be combined to have any efficacy.

The ways in which we pray are not specified, and although I like a louder and passion-filled prayer meeting, I can still enjoy the solitude and silence of just being with Jesus. Jesus often made solitude part of his walk, withdrawing privately to solitary, remote places, like heading up a mountainside (Matt. 14:23). To withdraw, in Greek is *anachóreó*, meaning to retire, to withdraw or to take refuge. Disciples are to do the same. The cost here is somehow to make the time in our ridiculously busy modern lifestyles, to be in relationship, walking and talking with Jesus. It may mean having to plan intentional time into the diary and even getting up out of your warm beds.

There is so much to pray for. Citizens will watch and pray. Praying for their leaders and others facing battles, whether fellow citizens or even our enemies. An army upholding each other in prayer. In the garden of Gethsemane just before Jesus is arrested, he asked his disciples to pray. Unfortunately, they fell asleep – it was in the middle of the night after all (Matt. 26:36-46). It is during the darkness that many of the enemy's schemes are implemented and so engaging the army in 24/7 prayer is always a great aim. Any natural war wages on into the night. As we intercede for others in prayer, we battle in the heavenly realms. As a pastor and church leader, I face spiritual battles daily, and sometimes they are intense! Your leaders need your prayers and a praying church will pray for them.

Consistency will also be needed as some battles take longer than others. Often too, our prayers are not always answered immediately. It took twenty years of praying with many friends and prayer partners from far-flung places all across this planet before God answered my prayer for a wife. God taught me much in those years and Alice was worth the wait!

Be Extravagant

"While Jesus was in Bethany in the home of Simon the Leper, [7] a woman came to him with an alabaster jar of very expensive perfume, which she poured on his head as he was reclining at the table. [8] When the disciples saw this, they were indignant. 'Why this waste?' they asked. [9] 'This perfume could have been sold at a high price and the money given to the poor.' [10] Aware of this, Jesus said to them, 'Why are you bothering this woman? She has done a beautiful thing to me. [11] The poor you will always have with you, but you will not always have me. [12] When she poured this perfume on my body, she did it to prepare me for burial. [13] Truly I tell you, wherever this gospel is preached throughout the world, what she has done will also be told, in memory of her'" (Matt. 26:6-13).

Jesus was often with outcasts, and on this occasion was in the house of a leper. An unnamed woman whose actions would be forever remembered (her story being recorded in all four gospels) was also there. She then pours out one of the most extravagant offerings, a jar full of highly valuable perfume. It was so valuable that it could have been a great help to the poor if it had been sold for its market value. We are fortunate to learn from those original twelve disciples. They get it wrong again and teach us something in the process. They considered first its monetary value and not its true purpose; the most highly valued perfume was used for the preparation of the burial of the most highly valued King. The woman had done a beautiful thing and given her greatest possession away, not wastefully, but purposefully and in the perfect timing. While the disciples were looking at the budget, she was worshipping the King (also see Luke 7:38).

The cost for us as citizens is that we should not ignore the poor and must consider them, but our best is given in extravagant worship to our King. Many are generous and give, but many more would not even consider giving a basic tithe, which was the OT form of giving at 10% of income. The NT teaches that everything we have is his and we must not hold onto every material thing that we possibly can in this life. For me, I gave up highly paid IT consultancy work to pastor a church with little finance, as just one example. How will you continue to be, or become, an extravagant giver? Who will you bless as an act of worship?

Never Betray

"Then one of the Twelve – the one called Judas Iscariot – went to the chief priests [15] *and asked, 'What are you willing to give me if I deliver him over to you?' So they counted out for him thirty pieces of silver.* [16]*From then on Judas watched for an opportunity to hand him over"* (Matt. 26:14-16).

It is only Matthew who records the actual amount or monetary value of the betrayal of Jesus. It is thought that each piece of silver could have been worth 120 days wages. Thirty times that equates to ten years of wages. A nice sum to have for a few minutes of betraying activity. What could we be tempted to do for ten years of salary? It is something 'not to be sniffed at'. If he can just make the deal happen, then he could retire early, or live the good life for a prolonged season.

"When evening came, Jesus was reclining at the table with the Twelve. ²¹ And while they were eating, he said, 'Truly I tell you, one of you will betray me.' ²² They were very sad and began to say to him one after the other, 'Surely you don't mean me, Lord?' ²³ Jesus replied, 'The one who has dipped his hand into the bowl with me will betray me. ²⁴ The Son of Man will go just as it is written about him. But woe to that man who betrays the Son of Man! It would be better for him if he had not been born'" (Matt. 26:20-24).

We cannot hide anything from God, so why do we even try. Jesus knew exactly who would betray him and yet in his love, Judas is not named and shamed. We can see that betrayal brings sadness. I'll say that again – betrayal brings sadness. The one who betrays will usually later on end up with regret and remorse; the one betrayed is often immediately left devastated. We hope that we would never do that to anyone let alone to Jesus. How is it then that so many citizens of the Kingdom have betrayed others or have been betrayed by those not yet in the Kingdom as well as by other citizens? So many are hurt by the church or by the actions of those within it. True citizens would never seek to intentionally betray Jesus or others. It is a very necessary addition to the life of every disciple.

Isn't it amazing that Jesus even allowed his betrayer to share his meal, during which they all 'took communion'? Today churches can exclude people from communion, or we might even disqualify ourselves because we feel unworthy to partake. Think about that for a moment.

The course of the events that would then follow had already been divinely orchestrated, and they would soon be publicly played out. A strong ending shows the severity of punishment that awaits those who choose throughout their lives to betray Jesus, by never actually accepting him. Disciples must remain loyal even if the other options presented seem more attractive.

Never Disown

"Then Jesus told them, 'This very night you will all fall away on account of me, for it is written: "'I will strike the shepherd, and the sheep of the flock will be scattered.'' 32 But after I have risen, I will go ahead of you into Galilee.' 33 Peter replied, 'Even if all fall away on account of you, I never will.' 34 'Truly I tell you,' Jesus answered, 'this very night, before the cock crows, you will disown me three times.' 35 But Peter declared, 'Even if I have to die with you, I will never disown you.' And all the other disciples said the same" (Matt. 26:31-35).

Disown means to give up ownership, deny or turn your back on what you stand for. This is something that citizens should never do in relation to their King Jesus and his Kingdom. What is it that caused all of the first disciples to scatter in fear and therefore essentially disown Jesus? We know for Peter this was three times a literal occurrence. However, that night they would all do just this, despite Jesus having given them the hope of his resurrection from the dead. Perhaps, as in the previous times, Jesus informed them that he would be tortured and killed (Matt. 16:21; 17:9, 23), they were simply unable to comprehend and take in what they were being told. Even with this additional attempt by Jesus, the disciple's actions do not match their intentions. They promise him, yet in this example, it is Peter saying he would never fall away from him, even if that meant death. Jesus says that Peter would disown him three times that same night. The others all made the same promise.

We can and do make promises that sometimes we are not able to keep. We say and really mean the things we say with every good intention, but then something dramatic happens and we fail to keep them. Failing to keep a promise is one thing, but denying Jesus is another. Perhaps this is what Jesus meant when had earlier taught his hearers to let their 'yes' be yes and their 'no' be no (Matt. 5:37). If we look at this mass denial of Jesus for those who had walked by his side for a little over three years, we could wonder if we would have any chance ourselves given the same circumstances. After receiving the Holy Spirit, however, they later became bold declarers and demonstrators of his Kingdom, with many of them being martyred for their unwavering faith. When we are filled with the Spirit and have the fuller revelation of Jesus and his Kingdom, we are then empowered to do the same. If we do deny Jesus then that too will end up with regret and tears (Matt. 26:75), but thank goodness we have a King who would willingly restore broken relationships (John 21:15-19).

Resist Temptation

"Watch and pray so that you will not fall into temptation. The spirit is willing, but the flesh is weak" (Matt. 26:41).

It is in the middle of a major crisis that the disciples give in to sleep, which represents the desires of the flesh, and they neglect to pray, which represents a failure to walk in the Spirit. If they cannot turn to God in prayer during crisis, how will they be able to do so when things are running more smoothly, when there is no pressure?

Citizens have to learn that at all times we take everything to God in prayer. We are to walk in the Spirit, doing the things the Spirit prompts us to do, flowing in spiritual gifts and growing in spiritual fruit. Sounds easy enough, but the reality is that we can struggle to pray even when life is easy and going well; "no need for the church prayer meeting this week I need time to relax and catch up on TV". That thought turns into reality all too frequently. We are to develop the habit of going to God in prayer. Then when the crisis comes are default behaviour is not to sleep, but to pray with great passion.

Think about the ways in which you have to resist ungodliness; the tempter will certainly tempt, but citizens resist and stay close to their King.

Be Truthful and never Gossip

"The chief priests and the whole Sanhedrin were looking for false evidence against Jesus so that they could put him to death. [60] But they did not find any, though many false witnesses came forward. Finally two came forward [61] and declared, 'This fellow said, "I am able to destroy the temple of God and rebuild it in three days."' [62] Then the high priest stood up and said to Jesus, 'Are you not going to answer? What is this testimony that these men are bringing against you?' [63] But Jesus remained silent (Matt. 26:59-63).

The ruling council of Israel were able to, and did, condemn Jesus. They were so hell-bent on reaching their desired verdict, to condemn Jesus, that they lost all perspective on truth. False accusation came from all angles. They were happy to hear this gossip but no case held together for this ruling to materialise. Until, that is, the two needed witnesses collaborated on the same untruthful story, because it was a truth taken out of context. Jesus saw through it all and knew simply to remain silent.

Citizens must always be truthful even if it will make them unpopular. We must never bend the truth, nor tell partial truth so that we might benefit. So much of this still happens in our lives through Christian friendships and even churches. If you struggle with speaking the truth personally or if you have been at the hand of those speaking falsely against you, then let me refer you back to the chapter on being authentic in section one. You may not be able to change having been on the receiving end of gossip, but you must walk in forgiveness and apply truth in all its fulness to your own life. It will benefit you, as well as others, as you become an authentic disciple.

Be Honouring

"*As evening approached, there came a rich man from Arimathea, named Joseph, who had himself become a disciple of Jesus. [58] Going to Pilate, he asked for Jesus' body, and Pilate ordered that it be given to him. [59] Joseph took the body, wrapped it in a clean linen cloth, [60] and placed it in his own new tomb that he had cut out of the rock. He rolled a big stone in front of the entrance to the tomb and went away. [61] Mary Magdalene and the other Mary were sitting there opposite the tomb*" (Matt. 27:57-61).

Joseph originally from another part of Israel (locale uncertain); was rich and owned a large estate in Jerusalem. He had become a disciple of Jesus and wished to use his wealth and influential position to honour Jesus in his death. He must have had influence to get an audience with Pilate. It is believed that the bodies of criminals would sometimes be handed over to friends for burial. He did what he was able to do, with what he had; he honoured Jesus and did the right thing.

This is all that Jesus asks of us. It does not matter if we have much or little, but we all have spiritual influence and must choose to use it to honour Jesus and to live lives that bear fruit for his Kingdom. This will cost us in both time and money. It is all about walking the narrow path after all. Things that are worthy, or in this case Jesus himself, simply deserve to be honoured. It means treating him with the greatest respect and fulfilling all our obligations to him, which will require courage, but will bring us freedom and the empowerment to reach our destiny in him. Honouring Jesus releases his life into our situation... *"Those who honour me I will honour"* (1 Sam. 2:30).

Have Joyful Expectation

"So the women hurried away from the tomb, afraid yet filled with joy, and ran to tell his disciples. ⁹ Suddenly Jesus met them. 'Greetings,' he said. They came to him, clasped his feet and worshipped him" (Matt. 28:8-9).

Suddenly things change. Hope and expectation had been lost with the realisation that the Saviour of Israel, and of the world, had died. It was all over. A couple of nights of sleep often help to bring us a better perspective on the things we may be facing, especially when the issues are drastic and potentially life-changing. After initial reactions and unbelief, the first disciples had now had a couple of nights of sleep. The reality of their lives moving ahead without their friend, leader, teacher and their God, had dawned. The women went to the tomb and were the first to encounter the risen Jesus, alive and well having overcome death. Joy beyond measure suddenly bursts forth, hope returns and expectations are instantly changed. They had no idea what this would all mean going forwards, but they become the first givers of the world's best news.

When Jesus suddenly appears as reality to us, our lives are changed around and become full of joy. As citizens of the Kingdom, we should always be expecting the new or the 'suddenly of God' – for Jesus to break in, in new and amazing ways. This is on both a personal level and on a gathered level i.e. at church or small groups. Jesus is still the King of the Kingdom, sitting at the right hand of Father God, waiting to return to this earth. All that we read about in the Bible can be the reality we experience in any gathering that embraces the Holy Spirit.

When his power comes and manifests suddenly among us, we can become disturbed by what might be happening, instead of willingly grasping all that is from God, and worshipping Jesus. Expectation costs us in our continual choice to walk with that kind of belief. To then be joyful and to worship in whatever God is doing, when the suddenly moments happen, can also be a costly choice.

In Conclusion

These additional items that we find in Matthew on the cost of discipleship could each have been a chapter in their own right, but I am not wanting to take us too far from our focus chapters eight, nine and ten. Despite not being exhaustive, my hope is that they will have added some new ingredients, enhancing the flavour of what we should be learning about, growing in, and helping others to also live out.

We have touched briefly on a number of critical issues: having faith, being good stewards, being humble, serving, prayer and intercession, extravagance, never to betray, never to disown, resisting temptation, being truthful and never gossiping, honouring and having joyful expectation. These are not to be optional extras that we simply pick and choose. None of these additional ingredients should be missed out, as they will bring greater health to our overall discipleship diet.

Salvation is free, discipleship will cost you your life!

In Summary

In this section 'The Making of a Disciple', the aim has been to show, from Matthew chapters eight, nine and ten, what it does mean to be a disciple. If we know this, then we know what we need to change in our own lives, but also what to help build into those that we are discipling. It was important to also pick up two further essentials for discipleship, journeying into Matthew chapter eleven to learn about 'seeking the Father', and chapter sixteen to see the necessity of 'taking up your cross.' Our voyage crossed over into Luke's Gospel to make sure we knew what would exclude us from being an effective disciple. Lastly, we scanned the rest of Matthew in a search for any additional costs that we should also be prepared to pay, in living for Jesus.

We have seen that this means many things:
- being convinced, willing and available (Matt. 4:18-22);
- being enthusiastic and without hesitation (Matt. 8:18-22);
- being obedient and merciful (Matt. 9:9-13);
- fasting (Matt. 9:14-17);
- going as authorised workers who demonstrate heaven (Matt. 9:37-10:8);
- being totally committed (Matt. 10:9-15);
- expecting opposition (Matt. 10:16-36);
- giving ultimate loyalty (Matt. 10:37-42);
- seeking the Father (Matt. 11:25-30);
- taking up your cross (Matt. 16:24-28);
- avoiding the essential cannot reasons (Luke 14:25-35);
- living the additional twelve costs (Matt. 17-28).

Yes, there is a cost to following Jesus, but it really is a small price to pay for the incredible adventure we can all live in this life, regardless of age or ability, living it in intimacy with our loving heavenly Father, our majestic saviour Jesus and in the very real presence of the Holy Spirit.

The spiritual Kingdom of Heaven manifests itself in the natural realm, not just in good deeds and service, but also in power! We cannot work through any gospel account and fail to see, believe and therefore expect the works of Jesus and his Kingdom to be demonstrated both in us and by us to others – in healings, deliverance and miracles as we go. The Spirit partners with us and plays the most significant part. Being a citizen will require much from you. A totally focused and committed pursuit of Jesus, and a complete willingness to be transformed into his likeness, as well as a heart that obediently serves him. There is no plan B.

Salvation is *still* free; discipleship will *still* cost you your life!

Epilogue

The requirements for citizens of the Kingdom are quite the discussion. After we truly grasp what our salvation means and what authentic discipleship is, then we can begin to see and understand its true cost and become someone who is willing to pay that price.

Matthew's 'Kingdom of Heaven' Gospel certainly holds the advice that we need. This knowledge, when placed upon the foundational framework of our inheritance (see the first book in this **Kingdom Perspective** series '*Territory of the Kingdom*'), allows us to comprehend more fully both the greatness of the Kingdom and the call of our King to live as one of its citizens, to be his subject.

This incredible Kingdom is conferred upon us as its **Citizens**, those who have entered its **Territory**, to live a life of great adventure. We achieve this through our willingness to live sacrificially for it and also by following its life-changing **Laws**. None of this is possible without having a deep, meaningful and ongoing relationship with our **King**: Jesus.

We are supposed to be on a mission to manifest the Kingdom of Heaven through demonstration and the making of authentic disciples of others. The ethics of the greatest ever Kingdom have to become our personal ethic and the way that we live. Kingdom thinking turns our thinking completely on its head. It is an upside-down Kingdom, which motivates and positions us to permeate the other kingdoms of this world.

I hope at the end of this second book in the series, that you are now able to see even more clearly, and perceive much more readily, the cost of living your life from a Kingdom Perspective.

Looking ahead, as true citizens who remain committed to being disciples ourselves, which requires us to make disciples of others, we now need to consider how we are to function and behave in the Kingdom that we have become a part of. Stay tuned, next up we will venture into the very heart of Jesus in...**Laws of the Kingdom**!

Bibliography

Barclay, W. The Gospel of Matthew Vol. 1. Edinburgh: The Saint Andrew Press, 1962.

_____,. The Gospel of Matthew Vol. 2. Edinburgh: The Saint Andrew Press, 1960.

_____,. The Gospel of Luke. Edinburgh: The Saint Andrew Press, 1960.

Berkhof, L. Systematic Theology. Edinburgh: The Banner of Truth Trust, 1958.

Black, J. Apostolic Theology. A Trinitarian Evangelical Pentecostal Introduction to Christian Doctrine. Luton: The Apostolic Church, 2016.

Bock, D. L. Luke Vol. 2: 9:51-24:53. Grand Rapids: Baker Academic, 1996.

Boice, J. M. Foundations of the Christian Faith. A Comprehensive & Readable Theology. Downers Grove: Inter-Varsity Press, 1986.

Bonhoeffer, D. The Cost of Discipleship. London: SCM Press, 1959.

Grudem, W. Systematic Theology. An Introduction to Biblical Doctrine. Leicester: Inter-Varsity Press, 1994.

Hoffbrand, D. The Jewish Jesus. Reconnecting with the truth about Jesus, Israel, & the Church. Shippensburg: Destiny Image Publishers Inc., 2017.

Hull, B., Sobels, B. The Discipleship Gospel. What Jesus preached – we must follow. USA: Harrington Interactive Media (HIM) Publications, 2018.

Ladd, G. E. A Theology of the New Testament. Grand Rapids: William B. Eerdmans Publishing Company, 1974.

_____,. The Gospel of the Kingdom. Popular Expositions on the Kingdom of God. Grand Rapids: WM. B. Eerdmans Publishing Co., 1959.

Lenski, R. C. H. The Interpretation of St. Matthew's Gospel. Commentary on the New Testament Series. Minneapolis: Augsburg Publishing House, 1961.

Miller, D. The Kingdom and the Power. The Kingdom of God: A Pentecostal Interpretation. Springfield: AIA Publications, 2008.

Milne, B. Know The Truth. A Handbook of Christian Belief. Leicester: Inter-Varsity Press, 1982.

Morris, L. Luke. An Introduction and Commentary. Tyndale New Testament Commentaries. Leicester: Inter-Varsity Press, 1980.

Pawson, D. Kingdoms in Conflict. Reading: Anchor Recordings Ltd., 2015

Slater, W. F. The Gospel of Saint Matthew. The Century Bible. Edinburgh: T.C. & E.C. Jack Ltd., 1901.

Tasker, R. V. G. Matthew. An Introduction and Commentary. Tyndale New Testament Commentaries. Leicester: Inter-Varsity Press, 1978.

Thiessen. H. C. Lectures in Systematic Theology. Grand Rapids: William B. Eerdmans Publishing Company, 1979.

Turner, D. L. Matthew. Baker Exegetical Commentary on the New Testament. Grand Rapids: Baker Publishing Group, 2008.

Warrington, K. Pentecostal Theology. A Theology of Encounter. London: T & T Clark, 2008.

Willard, D. The Divine Conspiracy. Rediscovering Our Hidden Life in God. London: William Collins, 1998.

_____,. Renovation of the Heart. Putting on the Character of Christ. Nottingham: Inter-Varsity Press, 2002.

Willard, D., Black, G. The Divine Conspiracy Continued. Fulfilling God's Kingdom on Earth. London: William Collins, 2014.

Author Biography

 Alan has been the Pastor at Elim Oasis Church, in Broadstairs, England since 2015. Having spent most of his Christian life as part of the Elim Pentecostal Church in the UK, he was then ordained as one of their ministers in 2014, after serving in numerous other Elim churches. Much of his time in ministry has been bi-vocational, working as an IT Software Consultant, alongside leading a church. He holds a BA Honours degree in Applied Theology and an MA degree in Pentecostal and Charismatic Theology, both from Regents Theological College in England.

His greatest desire is to make disciples of those who have chosen to follow Jesus. This has led him to begin this series of books, to help extend to others what he has learned from his own discipleship journey and his learning about the Kingdom, creating...**kingdomperspective.net** to make these resources available.

Alan has travelled widely and experienced mission in many nations, helping also to lead mission teams overseas, as well as hosting mission teams into the UK. He also helps by serving the Elim Missions department based in Malvern, England, both regionally and nationally.

Married to Alice, Alan is proud father to Carl married to Carly, Sasha married to Brook, and proud grandfather to four special granddaughters: Annabelle, Elowyn, Lucy and Eleanor.

Coming Soon

Lightning Source UK Ltd.
Milton Keynes UK
UKHW022015170122
397286UK00005B/66

9 781913 858025